A NEW SUBLIME

Piero Boitani

A NEW SUBLIME
TEN TIMELESS LESSONS
ON THE CLASSICS

*Translated from the Italian
by Ann Goldstein*

Europa
editions

Europa Editions
214 West 29th Street
New York, N.Y. 10001
www.europaeditions.com
info@europaeditions.com

Copyright © 2017 by Società editrice il Mulino, Bologna
First Publication 2020 by Europa Editions

Translation by Ann Goldstein
Original title: *Dieci lezioni sui classici*
Translation copyright © 2020 by Europa Editions

Library of Congress Cataloging in Publication Data is available
ISBN 978-1-60945-537-8

Boitani, Piero
A New Sublime. Ten Timeless Lessons on the Classics

Book design by Emanuele Ragnisco
www.mekkanografici.com

Cover image: detail from photograph by Effems (Wikimedia Commons)

Prepress by Grafica Punto Print – Rome

Printed in the USA

CONTENTS

A NEW SUBLIME

Preface

In the summer of 2016, over lunch in Bologna, Roberto Antonini and Brigitte Schwarz, of Swiss RSI Rete Due Radiotelevisione, asked if I would be willing to put together ten episodes on the classics, for their program *Laser*, in the fall. The episodes would be thirty to thirty-five minutes each, and by "classics" they meant the writers and literary works of classical antiquity. The choice of authors, passages, and themes would be mine, subject to their approval, naturally.

It was an interesting challenge: to contain in some three hundred minutes, or around five and a half hours, what I thought about the most beloved works of ancient literature, and explain it to a non-academic, general public that didn't necessarily know the texts. I agreed enthusiastically, and right away began to imagine an itinerary, which is the one in this book.

It seemed immediately obvious that I had to start with the *Iliad* and the *Odyssey*, not only because they are the oldest literary documents of Greek civilization but also because, at least in the versions that have come down to us, they are flawless poems, each completely different from the other, and yet both extraordinarily compelling: the one "direct and tragic," as Aristotle said, the other "complex" and dual, full of shifts, flashbacks, projections into the future; the first the work of a youthful and vigorous intelligence, as Pseudo-Longinus in *On the Sublime* insisted, the second that of an old man's genius, devoted to fables, in love with the marvelous. (The classics have the right to be judged by their own criteria, and that is why I use Aristotle and the anonymous author I will from now on call simply Longinus.)

Homer would of necessity be followed by the birth of thought in *mýthos* and logos. From Hesiod, who talks about the origins of the cosmos in mythical terms, to the pre-Socratics, who discuss origins in terms of natural elements (water, air, fire, earth), we see coming into play wonder, as Aristotle described it at the start of the *Metaphysics*: the wonder that is at the root of the love of knowledge, or philosophizing (which, in modern terms, indicates both philosophical thought and natural philosophy, or science), and of the love of myth, which means poetry and art. The pre-Socratics, who were the first to discuss being and becoming, are fascinating, partly because they appear to speak in enigmatic fragments. In general, though, they are not great poets, whereas Lucretius is a great poet and, centuries later, takes up their inheritance, combining it with the philosophy of Epicurus and influencing all the Latin poetry that follows, from Virgil to Ovid, Horace, and Manilius.

Fifth-century Greece suddenly, and almost simultaneously, sees the birth of history, philosophy, medicine, democracy, tragedy, and justice, and, a little earlier, the lyric, which replaces the "we" with the "I." These births are not always painless: knowledge, as Prometheus, Oedipus, and Socrates testify, is born in tragedy, in suffering and death. Tracking these developments, reading Herodotus and Thucydides, the *Oresteia* of Aeschylus and the *Electras* of Euripides and Sophocles, measuring the overreach of the giver of fire to men and the self-appointed detective who finds himself guilty, seeing a man die while he is talking about death and immortality—all that leads us to the classics. And from that man who calmly drinks the poison to which Athens has condemned him come Plato and Aristotle, who will dictate the philosophical agenda of the West for more than two thousand years.

The invention of Rome arrives later: the inhabitants of a small village on the Tiber persisted, steadily and with incredible success, for a thousand years. Virgil consecrates that invention when the village has become *Urbs* and *Orbis*, city and entire world, but Tacitus attacks its imperialistic foundations just as a new culture, the Christian, prepares to enter the scene. Ovid, the greatest ancient narrator after Homer, has on the other hands left us the poem of becoming and continuous transformation: the first great postmodern classic.

The ten episodes, which in the meantime had become "lessons," by choice of the publisher, could become twelve, twenty-four, thirty-six, if we were to explore—I don't know—comedy, the Alexandrian poets, the long period of slow decline. Classical antiquity lasts fifteen centuries, from Homer to Boethius, and contains enormous riches, although an unimaginable quantity of them are lost (of a hundred plays composed by Sophocles, to take one example, only seven have survived in their entirety). Ten was the just measure for a good challenge.

Fifteen hundred years, antiquity, and within it the classics. We know that the term goes back to Aulus Gellius, a Roman writer of the second century A.D., and author of the *Attic Nights*. Gellius uses the word "classic" to mean a writer "of class," as opposed to a "proletarian." The eminently "comparative" Greek and Latin canon of the classics, according to the testimony of Quintilian, includes, on the Greek side, Homer and Hesiod, Pindar, Simonides, and Callimachus, the tragic and comic writers, the historians, the orators and philosophers, and on the Latin Virgil and, among others, Ennius, Lucretius, Ovid, Horace, the tragic and comic writers, the historians, the orators, the philosophers (including Cicero and Seneca).

Quintilian's classics are also ours, almost two thousand years later. Or, rather, they are that special branch of classics, the classics par excellence, which we call the Classics, those of classical antiquity. Gradually, the Bible and the Christian writers have been absorbed into the larger canon of classics, along with writers from the Germanic areas of Europe, who were considered "barbarians," and those who from medieval times will be called "modern." Between the *Convivio*, *De Vulgari Eloquentia*, and the *Divine Comedy*, Dante produces his canons of authors ancient and modern. Shortly afterward, the Italian Humanists, who introduce the distinction between classical antiquity, Middle Ages, and Renaissance, rediscover a considerable quantity of lost ancient classics in the libraries of the Byzantine East: to be precise, in December of 1423 Giovanni Aurispa returns from Constantinople to Venice with two hundred and thirty-eight manuscripts, that is, the greater part of the Greek literature known to us—including the seven tragedies of Sophocles.

National canons of classics—that is, those originating in the various European languages—are codified later: for example, in Italian literature the Sicilian School, Stilnuovo, Dante, Petrarch, Boccaccio, the Humanists, Pulci, Boiardo, Ariosto, Tasso, Machiavelli, Guicciardini, and so on up to the twentieth century. This process continues today, when certain developments occur, or are occurring. First, a sort of international status of "classic" has been created for writers of the caliber of Homer, Dante, Shakespeare, Cervantes, and Goethe. Second, Chinese, Indian, Persian, and Arabic works and authors have entered the European canon, not to mention—slowly—those from countries formerly colonized by the Europeans. Finally, there is *Weltliteratur*, world or universal literature, which emerged after Goethe, who invented the term, and which has been gradually acquiring classics of its own.

Here, however, I have confined myself to the standard classics, those of antiquity, and not even all of them, limiting myself, rather, to beginnings, to "births," and to the early development of the most important genres. The greatest challenge lay in the medium itself: radio doesn't allow lengthy academic examinations, the talk has to be clear and absorbing, not bland, it has to use extensive quotations from the authors, and such passages should be read with passion and purpose. One should never, I think, read a prepared text, as if it were a communiqué from the White House. One should converse and improvise on the basis of notes. The ten episodes on the classics that the RSI broadcast (and which are available, under my name, on the site, https://bit.ly/2XO3A3T) conform to those requirements and had a modest success. But transforming them into a book—which someone (I no longer remember who) almost immediately proposed, and which the RSI generously permitted—is a rather different undertaking. There is no voice here reading about Hector dying or Polyphemus drunk such as filled the descriptive or critical gaps in the radio broadcast. Nor is it possible to express oneself through the use of interruptions and repetitions. A couple per page are more than enough. You have to speak in simple but articulate, complete sentences, as precise as possible, with a beginning and an end. The transcripts that the publisher provided of the ten original episodes made me despair: they couldn't be presented to an audience of readers. At most, they could be used as outlines and, every so often, as the source of a vivid turn of phrase.

That is what I did in rewriting the episodes for this book. I hope that they preserve a touch of their original freshness but are still readable.

And let's not forget Derek Walcott's caution: "The classics can console. But not enough."

Rome, June 2017

Piero Boitani

I
THE POEM OF FORCE AND PITY: THE *ILIAD*

Rage—Goddess, sing the rage of Peleus' son Achilles,
murderous, doomed, that cost the Achaeans countless losses,
hurling down to the House of Death so many sturdy souls,
great fighters' souls, but made their bodies carrion,
feasts for the dogs and birds,
and the will of Zeus was moving toward its end.
Begin, Muse, when the two first broke and clashed,
Agamemnon lord of men and brilliant Achilles.[1]

This is the opening of the *Iliad*: the first, and perhaps greatest, poem of the West, the first classic, with which our literature begins. Three thousand years ago, in the ninth century B.C., the "first Homer," as he's now called (the "second" is the Homer of the *Odyssey*), composes the poem of the Greeks' war against Troy. Maybe there wasn't a Homer and maybe the *Iliad* was originally simply a series of songs that were later collected and organized by someone. But it's nice to believe, as the ancient Greeks did, in a young blind bard who invented the *Iliad*: a story that has had countless rewritings in the European tradition, from Virgil's *Aeneid* to Tolstoy's *War and Peace*.

What to say about this poem? It's the poem of war, an account of the first "world war," we might call it, between East and West: Helen, the wife of Menelaus, the king of Sparta, is smitten with love for Paris, the son of Priam, and follows him to Troy, and to get her back the Greeks, from all the Achaean kingdoms, embark on an expedition to besiege Troy, in the hope of breaching the walls, destroying the city, and bringing Helen home to Sparta.

This war, as we know, lasted ten years, and ended with the capture of the city. The city was taken not by force, however, but by cunning. It's Odysseus who suggests the stratagem: the wooden horse inside which the strongest Greek warriors are concealed and which the Trojans will then bring into the city, to the acropolis, as a votive offering to Athena. At night, when the Trojans, having celebrated the end of the war, are asleep—and the Greek ships have sailed away and are hidden behind an island opposite the shore—the Greeks come out of the horse and slaughter the Trojans, burn the city, and carry off the women as slaves.

Yet this story of the taking of Troy is not in the *Iliad*. It is told, rather, in the *Odyssey* and narrated more fully later by Virgil, in the *Aeneid*, where Aeneas, one of the Trojans who have survived and fled, tells the story to Dido, the queen of Carthage. The *Iliad*, as the initial lines say, recounts only the preliminaries, the rage of Achilles—that is, the relatively brief period during which Achilles withdraws from active combat because he has quarreled with Agamemnon, who has seized his slave Briseis, his favorite concubine. But in that interval, dominated by the rage of Achilles, everything happens that is important and will later determine the conclusion of the war: because without Achilles, who is the strongest, most invincible, unrivalled among the Greek warriors, the Greeks lose, are forced to retreat, and are then chased back into their camp. Besides, their ships are not anchored offshore but drawn up onto the beach: if the Trojans can enter the Greek camp and burn the ships, they've won the war. And in fact at a certain point they are about to do just that, because Priam's son Hector, who is the strongest of the Trojan fighters, leads his troops almost to the Greek camp, halting because night falls. If Hector had continued the attack, he would have accomplished a real Blitzkrieg (literally, lightning war) and vanquished the Greeks.

When the battle resumes, the next morning, the Greeks can't withstand the assault and are killed or put to flight. Then Patroclus, the inseparable companion of Achilles, implores his friend to let him fight in his place. Achilles gives Patroclus his own armor and Patroclus descends to the field. He is challenged and killed by Hector, who carries off the armor. Now Achilles, seized not by anger, which is what he feels toward Agamemnon, but by blind, almost bestial fury, inspired by his friendship for and attachment to Patroclus, rejoins the battle, receiving new weapons and armor, made specially by Hephaestus. Achilles pursues Hector three times around the walls of the city, fights a final duel with him, and kills him. The end of Hector is in fact the end of Troy. There is no use recounting the capture of the city: once Hector is eliminated, Troy, sooner or later, will fall.

Achilles mutilates Hector's body, but the gods won't allow it to be ruined or to decompose. The poem concludes with Priam, the old king, Hector's father, going alone to Achilles' tent to recover his son's body: a moment of great, intense emotion. Invoking the affection that Achilles feels for his own father, Peleus, and offering the hero an enormous ransom, Priam manages to get his son's body and gain a truce to celebrate the funeral rites. This is what marks the end of the poem.

There is no doubt, therefore, that the *Iliad*, this compact, direct, terrible, and tragic poem, as Aristotle said in the *Poetics*, is a song of war: "the poem of force," Simone Weil maintained. Not one of the twenty-four books into which it was organized, by Alexandrian grammarians, lets us forget the clash of arms, obscures the fact that force is "the true hero, the true subject matter, the center" of the poem. "The force that men wield," Weil wrote, "force that subdues men, force in the face of which human flesh shrinks back": force that "makes a thing of whoever submits to it." The many battles, the countless duels of the *Iliad* are, one might say, the transcription, or the song, of a world (of men and gods, who also take part in the conflict) that believes in force, loves it and thinks that everything can be resolved by means of it: in short, the mirror of a cosmic conflict, flashes of which can be glimpsed the moment Achilles returns to the field.

Perhaps it's appropriate that the first literary work of our tradition is devoted to war and to force: two things that accompanied us until a few decades ago, and have made the history of *Homo sapiens* a bloody one. The first thinkers were aware of this. In the *Theogony*, Hesiod, leaving aside concrete fighting, places Eris—strife, conflict—at the start of the cosmos, generated by Night. Later, Heraclitus speaks of *pólemos*, war: "*Pólemos* is the father of all things and is king of all things"; "Everything happens following the law of strife (*éris*) and necessity." Even Empedocles, though he has the opposite point of view, maintains the fundamental importance of *néikos*, struggle. Further, the *Iliad* itself has been seen as "agonistic." Writing in the second century A.D., Longinus describes it as "dramatic" and "made of conflict" (*enagónion*), and, recalling a passage in Book XV, says that Homer is swept along in the whirlwind of the struggle: that he "shares in the inspiration of the fray, and is affected by it just as if he himself 'is raging madly, like Ares the spear-hurler, or as when ruinous flames rage among the hills, in the thickets of a deep forest, and foam gathers about his lips.'"[2]

The Ukrainian-born philosopher Rachel Bespaloff, in her essay *On the Iliad*,[3] also recognizes that force plays the central role in the poem, but, penetrating deep into its heart, she finds some moments of respite in which becoming—war—coagulates for a moment into being. The first of these is near the beginning of the poem, in Book III, when Greeks and Trojans agree to resolve the conflict by holding a duel between the two principal rivals, Menelaus, Helen's husband, and Paris, the Trojan who seized her and carried her off with him. The winner will get the woman, and the others will accept the result without objecting. The two begin to fight, but at a certain point the goddess Aphrodite, fearing that Menelaus will kill Paris, wraps him in a veil of cloud and transports him to his rooms in the royal palace of Troy.

At the beginning of the episode, Iris, the messenger of the gods, descends to earth in mortal guise to warn Helen, who has remained in the palace, that Menelaus and Paris are about to fight for her and urges her to go to the city walls to watch. Helen is weaving a great dark-red-colored robe, into which she works "the endless struggles" that Trojans and Achaeans confront "all for her at the god of battle's hands." Helen, in other words, is weaving the war of Troy and the *Iliad* while she lives them: as if the robe were a diary of war in fabric, a tapestry journal. The poem—and reality—is mirrored in distant and prismatic backdrops, opening an abyss that was observed, naturally, by Borges.

Helen, in whom Iris has inspired "yearning warm and deep" for her first husband, her parents, and her city, rushes to the walls, "cloaking herself in shimmering linen," and "live tears welling." The old people of Troy are sitting on the ramparts, "long years" having "brought their fighting days to a halt," but, Homer says, "eloquent speakers still, clear as cicadas settled on treetops, lifting their voices through the forest." As soon as they see Helen climbing up toward the tower, the old people quietly exchange "winged" words:

Who on earth could blame them? Ah, no wonder
the men of Troy and Argives under arms have suffered
years of agony all for her, for such a woman.
Beauty, terrible beauty!
A deathless goddess—so she strikes our eyes!
But still,
ravishing as she is, let her go home in the long ships
and not be left behind . . . for us and our children
down the years an irresistible sorrow.

The old people of Troy are struck by Helen, by her beauty—her "terrible" (the original text says *ainós*) beauty, similar to that of the immortals. Helen's beauty is not a blessing; it's a curse. And she knows it very well, immediately blaming herself for being the cause of the war.

There, that's a pause, a respite. Behind the war—that is, becoming—we glimpse being, and being is beauty. It's worthwhile to fight a war for beauty! Not for the conquest of Troy, for possession of the Dardanelles and access to the Black Sea, which is why the prosaic wars of modern Europe have been waged. No: to win supreme, inexpressible, divine beauty, the beauty of the immortal goddesses. It's worth the pain of "suffering agonies"! For a woman like that.

Even though these old people are dazzled by Helen, they would like to return her to the Greeks, but Priam, calling her over, absolves her of guilt and blames the gods instead: and he asks her the names of the Greek warriors who are moving down there, outside the Scaean Gates, waiting for the duel: Agamemnon, Odysseus, Ajax, Idomeneus. All powerful, mighty, strong: all, precisely, an expression of the ideal of force that dominates the poem. One of them, however, is a very skillful speaker: Odysseus. Old Antenor remembers him during a diplomatic mission with Menelaus years before, when they came to ask for the return of Helen:

But when Odysseus sprang up, the famed tactician would just stand
    there,
staring down, hard, his eyes fixed on the ground,
never shifting his scepter back and forth,

clutching it stiff and still like a mindless man.
You'd think him a sullen fellow or just plain fool.
But when he let loose that great voice from his chest
and the words came piling on like a driving winter blizzard—
then no man alive could rival Odysseus! Odysseus . . .
we no longer gazed in wonder at his looks.

Thus the pause that embodies "being" in feminine beauty yields to masculine power, and glides finally onto words. And that passage from one side to the other, from the city of the Trojans to those who besiege it and want to destroy it, doesn't allow admiration for the enemy to decrease by a single degree.

The first pause we encounter in Book VI is of a completely different nature. Book V recounts the deeds of Diomedes, a warrior so bold that he challenges the gods themselves and wounds Aphrodite, who has come to the aid of her son Aeneas. The battle rages again in Book VI, when Diomedes encounters Glaucus, the most courageous of the Trojans. Before the duel begins, Diomedes asks his adversary what his lineage is. He doesn't want to fight with a god, he declares. Glaucus answers with a famous speech:

The noble son of Hippolochus answered staunchly,
"High-hearted son of Tydeus, why ask about my birth?
Like the generations of leaves, the lives of mortal men.
Now the wind scatters the old leaves across the earth,
now the living timber bursts with the new buds
and spring comes round again. And so with men:
as one generation comes to life, another dies away."

What's the use of knowing a man's lineage (*geneé*), if it's like that of the leaves? That is, fundamentally transient, intrinsically fragile, fleeting. It should be noted that Glaucus speaks of human *lineages*, not of single individuals, as, we'll see, lyric poetry does. He compares families, houses (lineages), and generations of human beings to leaves. Homer is thinking not of the single leaf but of the foliage of an entire tree, in fact the leaves of an entire forest. He draws a universal panorama: the panorama of continuous becoming.

But the scene isn't over. Glaucus in effect answers Diomedes by stating his entire descent, with the slowness, fullness, and precision that Homer reserves for such things. And then the adversary is pleased: because he discovers that his grandfather Oineus once received in his house Bellerophon, Glaucus' grandfather:

"Splendid—you are my friend,
my guest from the days of our grandfathers long ago! . . .
Come, let us keep clear of each other's spears,
even there in the thick of battle. Look,
plenty of Trojans there for me to kill,
your famous allies too, any soldier the god
will bring in range or I can run to ground.
And plenty of Argives too—kill them if you can.
But let's trade armor. The men must know our claim:
we are sworn friends from our fathers' days till now!"

The relationship of hospitality (*xenía*) is sacred and protected by Zeus. In a world of constant potential enmity, it surpasses the *pólemos* that dominates everything, makes conversation and exchange with the other possible: it is a guarantee of human community, of civility. If the lineages and generations of men are like the leaves, hospitality is like the tree solidly planted, strongly rooted, in the earth: not eternal but lasting.

The encounter between Glaucus and Diomedes constitutes a very short truce, and therefore a pause, within the war. It's not a pause that, in the heart of becoming, reveals for a moment "being" but one that for an instant offers a window onto ethics. The pause that the rest of Book VI portrays is different again, with Hector returning briefly to the city and meeting his mother, Hecuba, his brother Paris, and Helen; his wife, Andromache, and his son Astyanax. What opens up here is a view into the besieged city, while at the same time the "familial," human side of the warrior Hector is developed: he is the only character in the entire *Iliad* of whom Homer describes not only his heroism but also his *philía*, his relationships at home, the love of his family.

Hector hurries through Troy and first encounters Hecuba, whom he urges to go to the temple of Athena to ask for the goddess's protection (which she denies her). Then he goes looking for Paris, and reproaches him bitterly for his absence from the battlefield. With him is Helen, who says of herself, "bitch that I am, vicious, scheming," for having followed Paris, but she holds the gods responsible for "this misfortune," and in particular Zeus. With that paradoxical vision of the relationship between divinities, tragic events, and poetry that we'll find again in the *Odyssey*, she declares, "Zeus planted a killing doom within us both, so even for generations still unborn we will live in song."

Finally Hector reaches his own house. But his wife, Andromache, isn't there: with her son and the nurse she has gone to the ramparts to see the outcome of the fighting, which she has been told has been deadly for the Trojans. Hector rushes along the streets and comes to the Scaean Gates. Andromache hurries toward him:

She joined him now, and following in her steps
a servant holding the boy against her breast,
in the first flush of life, only a baby,
Hector's son, the darling of his eyes
and radiant as a star . . .
Hector would always call the boy Scamandrius,
townsmen called him Astyanax, Lord of the City,
since Hector was the lone defense of Troy.
The great man of war breaking into a broad smile,
his gaze fixed on his son, in silence. Andromache,
pressing close beside him and weeping freely now,
clung to his hand, urged him, called him: "Reckless one,
my Hector—your own fiery courage will destroy you!
Have you no pity for him, our helpless son? Or me,
and the destiny that weighs me down, your widow,
now so soon? Yes, soon they will kill you off,
all the Achaean forces massed for assault, and then,
bereft of you, better for me to sink beneath the earth.
What other warmth, what comfort's left for me,
once you have met your doom? Nothing but torment!
I have lost my father. Mother's gone as well.

Andromache continues to beg Hector not to return to the battle. If he has to die, she will be left alone. She has no one in the world, because her father and brothers were killed by Achilles, and her mother is dead. For her, she says, Hector is father, brother, mother, and "splendid husband." But Hector responds like this:

All this weighs on my mind too, dear woman.
But I would die of shame to face the men of Troy
and the Trojan women trailing their long robes
if I would shrink from battle now, a coward.
Nor does the spirit urge me on that way.
I've learned it all too well. To stand up bravely,
always to fight in the front ranks of Trojan soldiers,
winning my father great glory, glory for myself.

Hector is deeply aware of duty, of the opinion of others, and of his own glory: he can't shirk, not him, nor could he bear the shame he would feel if he did. Finally, he can't evade the call of *kléos*, the glory that is linked to his name and that uniquely assures survival after death. (The Greeks of the archaic period believe in a Hades, another world, where they are only shadows, and think that securing glory for themselves is the only way to be remembered by future generations: everyone, during the Trojan War, fights to keep his *kléos* alive.) Anyway, Hector knows too well that "the day will come when sacred Troy must die, Priam must die and all his people with him." He is anguished about this, and thinking of his wife, in particular, who, when he is dead, will be dragged into slavery by some Achaean, and someone, seeing her weep, will say: "There is the wife of Hector, the bravest fighter they could field, those stallion-breaking Trojans, long ago when the men fought for Troy." "No, no, let the earth come piling over my dead body before I hear your cries, I hear you dragged away!" Hector exclaims. And he holds out his arms to take his son. But the father is still wearing his armor and helmet, whose crest jiggles with every movement, and the child, frightened, turns crying toward the safe breast of his nurse. Andromache and Hector laugh, Hector takes off the helmet, holds his son in his arms, rocks him and kisses him, praying to Zeus and all the gods to make Astyanax glorious so that one day someone will say that he is "a better man than his father." Then he puts the child in his mother's arms, and she welcomes him to her breast, crying and laughing at the same time (the original, made up of an adverb and a past participle, *dakruóen gelásasa,* has an extraordinary emotional force). Hector pities her, strokes her with his hand, and urges her to go back to the house and devote herself to her tasks, reminding her, in consolation, that no one has ever escaped his fate, and that no one can send him down to Hades against *móira,* fate. So he takes his helmet again and goes off toward the gates of the city, while Andromache, crying bitter tears and turning back frequently, goes home and, with her handmaidens, begins the lament. "So in his house they raised the dirges for the dead, for Hector still alive," Homer concludes.

It's an incredibly moving scene: an instant of peace within the war, but of peace dominated by the hammering thought of war, by the awareness, on her part and his, that this war will continue, and that it will probably lead to the death of Hector and the end of Troy. The shadow looms over Hector from that moment, and the mention of glory and fate in the same passage confers on him great psychological and, so to speak, theological depth. "The concern," the French philologist Jacqueline de Romilly writes in her book *Hector*, "with celebrating a hero from the enemy camp, with arousing pity for a defeated man, a man vowed to death and torture after death, that concern with showing a man who is discouraged by war, and whose death sows a lacerating sorrow, constitutes, on the threshold of Western literature, an evocation of extraordinary humanity. In our time of wars and massacres carried out in the name of religion or race, of cruelties sometimes continued after death and unexpectedly revealed by the discovery of depositories of bones, the rise of such humanity, in its simple and magisterial affirmation, is an answer to our anguish."[4] Hector, this longer pause in Book VI reminds us, has a mother, a wife, a son: like all of us, and more than any other fighter in the Trojan War, he has a family that conflicts with his commitment to war and his search for glory. And he can devote only a few minutes to it. The shield that Hephaestus makes for Achilles, in Book XVIII, portrays a prosperous, happy city, at peace, and one besieged, at war. It doesn't seem possible for one to exist without the other. But if there is someone in the *Iliad* who could forcefully affirm the profound need for the first—the city at peace—it is Hector.

Before returning to Hector and the end of the *Iliad*, I would like to linger for a moment on two of the images in the poem. The divinities, of course, intervene in the war, arrayed on one side or the other: Aphrodite, Ares, Apollo, Artemis with the Trojans; Hera, Athena, Poseidon, Hephaestus with the Greeks. The participation of the gods in the conflict was an "outrage," one of the main reasons that Plato accused Homer of being a liar and therefore excluded him from the republic of philosophers. It was also one of the reasons that, at the end of the sixth century B.C., Theagenes of Rhegium came up with an allegorical interpretation of the Homeric poems (Poseidon=water; Hera=air; Hephaestus=fire). But not everything that regards the gods in the *Iliad* is comic. Homer points out twice, in Book XIV, how Ocean was the "genesis," that is generator, father, of the gods. In the preceding book, we find a memorable image of Poseidon coming down to the sea, and Troy, from the highest peak of Samothrace:

Suddenly down from the mountain's rocky crags
Poseidon stormed with giant, lightning strides
and the looming peaks and tall timber quaked
beneath his immortal feet as the sea lord surged on.
Three great strides he took, on the fourth he reached his goal,
Aegae port where his famous halls are built in the green depths,
the shimmering golden halls of the god that stand forever.
Down Poseidon dove and yoked his bronze-hoofed horses
onto his battle-car, his pair that raced the wind
with their golden manes streaming on behind them,
and strapping the golden armor round his body,
seized his whip that coils lithe and gold
and boarded his chariot launching up and out,
skimming the waves, and over the swells they came,
dolphins leaving their lairs to sport across his wake,
leaping left and right—well they knew their lord.
And the sea heaved in joy, cleaving a path for him,
and the team flew on in a blurring burst of speed,
the bronze axle under the war-car never flecked with foam,
the stallions vaulting, speeding Poseidon toward Achaea's fleet.

This passage is cited by Longinus as one of those in which Homer "represents the divine nature as it really is, pure, majestic, and undefiled," and which is comparable to the passage describing the creation of light in the book of Genesis. The modern reader will find in it at least three principal moments. First, Poseidon's steps cover in an instant the distance that separates him from his goal, and at the same time make the peaks and the timber quake. Second, when the god reaches the Aegean, everything turns gold: the palace, the horses' manes, the armor, the whip. Third, the course of Poseidon in his battle-car toward the cave between Tenedos and Imbros, opposite Troy, isn't a simple ride but, rather, a flight on the crest of the waves: while the marine monsters play and the sea opens joyously, the chariot doesn't even touch the water—it skims it. First we see a series of giant steps that shake the mountains and the forest (Poseidon, Homer reminds us some lines later, is he who "grips and shakes the earth"), then a flash of gold on the sea. Longinus is right: it's sublime.

Another example, cited by the same author, concerns the flight of Hera in Book V. Here Zeus himself urges his wife to incite Athena, "the Predator," against Ares. Hera obeys Zeus' suggestion right away: she whips the horses, who take flight, "careering between the earth and the starry skies":

<blockquote>
as far
as a man's glance can pierce the horizon's misting haze,
a scout on a watchtower who scans the wine-dark sea—
so far do the soaring, thundering horses of the gods leap at a single
    stride.
</blockquote>

"But see how Homer exalts the heavenly powers," the author of *On the Sublime* comments. "He measures their mighty leap in terms of cosmic distances. Might one not exclaim, from the supreme grandeur of this, that if the steeds of the gods make two leaps in succession they will no longer find room on the face of the earth?" So this, too, is sublime.

The third episode is a true pause. There is a moment in the *Iliad* when the Trojans are about to win the war. Besieged, they have taken the battle, under Hector's leadership, to the plain between the city and the sea, and so toward the shore where the Greeks have beached their ships. In vain do the Greeks construct a wall to defend their encampment. At dawn, after a brief truce for the burial of the dead, the battle resumes furiously. When the sun "stood striding at high noon," Zeus holds out his golden scale, gripping it in the middle, and the fate of the Achaeans goes down, while that of the Trojans goes "lifting toward the sky." The greatest of the gods thunders from the summit of Ida and hurls a lightning bolt at the Greek army. Agamemnon, Idomeneus, the two Ajaxes can no longer stand their ground, and even Odysseus runs toward the ships. For a moment Diomedes resists, then he, too, is forced by Zeus to retreat.

Hector rages, leading the Trojans to the Greek rampart. Hera and Athena try to help the Greeks, but Zeus, angry, stops them, for the first time hinting openly at the plan he has in mind: to get Patroclus, Achilles' friend, to join the fight and be killed by Hector, so that Achilles, abandoning his own anger, will return to the field and, eliminating

Hector, give a decisive turn to the war. The Trojans continue to advance, but the sun dives into Ocean with its shining rays, "drawing the dark night across the grain-giving earth." Hector then musters his men and addresses them: they must obey "the dark night" (at night, according to the ethos of the *Iliad*, there is no fighting), prepare dinner, with food and wine brought from Troy, light fires to keep the Greeks from secretly slipping away. Then, in the morning, the attack will resume and will be decisive. The Trojans cheer, they unbridle the horses, have bread, cows, sheep, and wine transported from the city, gather wood, light fires, roast the meat.

The Trojans' "spirits soared as they took positions down the passageways of battle all night long." Watchfires are lighted, as the last lines of Book VIII describe:

Hundreds strong, as stars in the night sky glittering
round the moon's brilliance blaze in all their glory
when the air falls to a sudden, windless calm . . .
all the lookout peaks stand out and the jutting cliffs
and the steep ravines and down from the high heavens bursts
the boundless bright air and all the stars shine clear
and the shepherd's heart exults—so many fires burned
between the ships and the Xanthus' whirling rapids
set by the men of Troy, bright against their walls.

It's an extraordinary simile. Homer could have confined himself to saying, functionally (as the Bible does, as do so many others): there were as many fires as there are stars in the sky. Instead, he composes an incomparable nocturne, which opens up gradually to the infinite. First he sketches the stars shining around the luminous moon, then the windless air, then the silhouettes: a horizon, a border: cliffs, peaks, and valleys. And then a leap: the air becomes "boundless," infinite ("inexpressible," in the original), the stars return, all bright and clear, and an unexpected observer suddenly appears: a shepherd, who has little to do with war. He rejoices in his soul: because, we imagine, he looks at the spectacle of the sky and takes pleasure in it.

The presence of the observer introduces into the simile a proto-aesthetic perception, the joy of beauty, or, rather, of the sublime: because infinity, beyond the rocks and valleys, and ineffability are features typical not of the beautiful but, as Longinus observes, centuries later, of the sublime. Which lifts the heart, expands it, makes it vibrate. We understand why this image fascinated the poet Giacomo Leopardi when he discovered it in the poem, reading it in Greek at the age of eleven. He mentions it in *Ricordi* (*Recollections*), where he says it's equal to the "night view with the moon and clear sky from the height of his house just as in Homer's simile." He discusses it in *Discorso di un italiano sulla poesia romantica* (*Discourse of an Italian on Romantic Poetry*), in which it becomes the model of "senti-mental poetry." He is inspired by it in *Sappho's Last Song*, in *Evening of the Holiday*, in *Night Song of a Wandering Shepherd in Asia*. But what is it doing in the *Iliad*, the poem of war and force? It serves, we understand, to sketch a cos-mos where harmony rules, not strife. Maybe it's bound to that sky toward which, just at the beginning of Book VIII, the fate of the Trojans is "lifting" in Zeus's scale: and here besides the Trojans' "spirits soared." But maybe it also constitutes the only true pause in the *Iliad*, the only moment of respite, when the noise of warlike becoming truly recedes from the combatants, men and gods, and becomes the silence of nocturnal light, astral quiet: in which a single human being participates with joy, as far from Achilles, Odysseus, Agamemnon, Hector, Aeneas as they are from their servants and slaves—a humble shepherd, representative of a race that has nothing to do with a war of princes.

The vision of the cosmos has a fundamental importance in the *Iliad*. When Patroclus is killed, and Achilles decides to rejoin the battle, he needs new weapons, because Hector took the old ones, stripping the corpse of Patroclus. In Book XVIII of the *Iliad*, Achilles' mother, Thetis, implores Hephaestus to forge them. The gods' smith sets to work and produces first a marvelous shield. On it, as if it were a mirror of the world, he dramatically portrays two cities (one flourishing, at peace, where a trial is celebrated; the other besieged, gripped by the terrors of war) and the countryside, with herds, flocks, vineyard, musicians, and dancers. All around, along the outer rim of the shield, as if enclosing this human Earth, Hephaestus places the mighty current of the river Ocean. But the first thing the god carves into the shield of Achilles is the cosmos, as Book XVIII details:

There he made the earth and there the sky and the sea
and the inexhaustible blazing sun and the moon rounding full
and there the constellations, all that crown the heavens,
the Pleiades and the Hyades, Orion in all his power too
and the Great Bear that mankind also calls the Wagon:
she wheels on her axis always fixed, watching the Hunter,
and she alone is denied a plunge in the Ocean's baths.

Hephaestus portrays the entire universe on the shield: the earth and the sea, the sky, with the moon, the sun, and the stars assembled in constellations, making a crown for the sky. Among these is the Great Bear, which never sets in the northern sky and which to the Greeks of the ninth and eighth centuries B.C. serves as a reference point, in place of our North Star, in the Lesser Bear. The shield of Achilles places the cosmic gaze of archaic Greece in the foreground. It has the destroyer hero wear that cosmos, as he prepares to kill Hector, creating no less a paradox than the one presented by the simile of the stars when the battle stops for the night in Book VIII. The universe shines infinite in that suspended moment when Hector stops fighting: now Achilles will carry the entire universe into battle. In fact at the start of Book XXII, his armor will shine, like that of Diomedes before him, and like Orion's Dog, when, from the height of the walls, Priam watches as he begins his pursuit of Hector. Achilles is Sirius, the bright star that brings down on men "such killing fever."

Thus we reach the decisive moments of the *Iliad*, when Achilles returns to fight because Hector has killed his companion Patroclus. His re-entry onto the battlefield is marked by a universal conflagration: even the gods, in Book XX, take part in the fray, while Eris, Strife, incites the armies. Achilles now puts aside the *ménis*, the baleful rage against Agamemnon which up to now has dominated events in the *Iliad*. He is invaded instead by a boundless fury, a radical disdain for man, a desire for annihilation of the other that have no equal in Western literature. He attacks Hector once, but Apollo protects the Trojan. Then Achilles slaughters all the enemy soldiers he encounters, like a violent fire "raging on through the mountain gorges splinter-dry, setting ablaze big stands of timber, the wind swirling the huge fireball left and right." There is no longer anything human about him: he's a *dáimon*. He shows no mercy, overpowering everything before him, without restraint, until he is fighting with the river, Scamander, which pours over him, boiling. Hera goads Hephaestus to attack the river: fire against water, in a primordial clash of elements. The gods insult one another, mock one another, wound one another, while the Trojans, terrified, rush to seek refuge in the city.

The scene is set: Hector remains alone outside the walls waiting for Achilles, while his father and mother, Priam and Hecuba, who observe the events from above, beg him to return. But Hector stands firm, waiting, and yet doubtful in his mind, wondering if it wouldn't be better to go unarmed to meet his enemy and offer to give back Helen and the riches that Paris hauled away with her, and still more that could be collected in the city. But there's "no way to parley with that man—not now—not from behind some oak or rock to whisper, like a boy and a young girl, lovers' secrets a boy and girl might whisper to each other." Better to confront the fight.

So he wavered,
waiting there, but Achilles was closing on him now
like the god of war, the fighter's helmet flashing,
over his right shoulder shaking the Pelian ash spear,
that terror, and the bronze around his body flared
like a raging fire or the rising, blazing sun.

Hector looked up, saw him, started to tremble,
nerve gone, he could hold his ground no longer,
he left the gates behind and away he fled in fear—
and Achilles went for him, fast, sure of his speed
as the wild mountain hawk, the quickest thing on wings,
launching smoothly, swooping down on a cringing dove
and the dove flits out from under, the hawk screaming
over the quarry, plunging over and over, his fury
driving him down to beak and tear his kill—
so Achilles flew at him, breakneck on in fury
with Hector fleeing along the walls of Troy,
fast as his legs would go.

Hector flees and Achilles can't catch him, but the other
can't escape, either: Achilles prevents him from re-entering
the city through the Scaean Gates. It's almost like the paint-
ing of a chase, or the nightmare of a flight. It becomes a
very brief pause, a suspension in time, in the psyche, in a
dream:

endless as in a dream . . .
when a man can't catch another fleeing on ahead
and he can never escape nor his rival overtake him—
so the one could never run the other down in his speed
nor the other spring away.

The gods, however, are ready to intervene yet again in
the affairs of men. The two warriors have already com-
pleted three circuits around the walls of Troy when Zeus
complains that the fate of Hector is now sealed, that he will
lose one dear to him, one who offered him great, opulent
sacrifices. Athena, who sides with the Greeks, immediately

darkens: "What are you saying? A man, a mere mortal, his doom sealed long ago? You'd set him free from all the pains of death?" In the harsh theology of the *Iliad*, not even the Father of all the gods can break the decrees of Fate. Zeus doesn't resist, and now allows his daughter to do as she wishes. When Achilles and Hector reach the two fountains outside the walls of Troy for the fourth time, and Achilles signals to his men not to go against his enemy, Zeus takes his golden scales and weighs the fate of the two warriors. Hector's side descends inexorably downward. Now not even Zeus, not even if he wanted to, can do anything for him.

To smooth the path for Achilles' victory, Athena, the goddess of intelligence and cunning, appears on the battlefield in the guise of Deiphobos, one of Hector's brothers, to help him. Hector, refreshed, halts: he stops his flight and faces Achilles openly. He suggests to his adversary a pact by which whoever wins the duel will possess the arms of the other but will not damage the body and will return it to his people. Achilles refuses: pacts are not made between men and lions, between lambs and wolves. And he hurls his spear, which Hector manages to avoid. It's Hector's turn, he throws his: it rebounds off Achilles' formidable shield. Hector doesn't have another spear in reserve. He calls loudly to Deiphobos to bring him one, but his brother has disappeared. So Hector understands that the gods have deceived him and that the hour of his death has arrived.

It's the final clash between the two: the one, Hector, a great fighter and a man to his core; the other, Achilles, an even stronger warrior but, above all, relentless machine of war, "bursting with rage, barbaric" and unstoppable. Achilles advances with the spear in hand, observing his adversary's body in search of the exposed spot where he is vulnerable. The point of his spear gives off fire, "bright as that star amid the stars in the night sky, star of the evening, brightest star that rides the heavens." The armor that Hector took from Patroclus covers him entirely, except at the throat, where the collarbone divides the neck from the shoulder. Achilles aims at that spot and pierces the neck through, without cutting the trachea, so that he can respond to him. Hector falls:

he crashed in the dust—
godlike Achilles gloried over him:
"Hector—surely you thought when you stripped Patroclus' armor
that you, you would be safe! Never a fear of me—
far from the fighting as I was—you fool!
Left behind there, down by the beaked ships
his great avenger waited, a greater man by far—
that man was I. And I smashed your strength! And you—
the dogs and birds will maul you, shame your corpse
while Achaeans bury my dear friend in glory!"
Struggling for breath, Hector, his helmet flashing,
said, "I beg you, beg you by your life, your parents—
don't let the dogs devour me by the Argive ships!
Wait, take the princely ransom of bronze and gold,
the gifts my father and noble mother will give you—
but give my body to friends to carry home again,
so Trojan men and Trojan women can do me honor
with fitting rites of fire once I am dead."
Staring grimly, the proud runner Achilles answered,
"Beg no more, you fawning dog—begging me by my parents!

Would to god my rage, my fury would drive me now
to hack your flesh away and eat you raw—
such agonies you have caused me! Ransom?
No man alive could keep the dog-packs off you,
not if they haul in ten, twenty times that ransom
and pile it here before me and promise fortunes more—
no, not even if Dardan Priam should offer to weigh out
your bulk in gold! Not even then will your noble mother
lay you on your deathbed, mourn the son she bore . . .
The dogs and birds will rend you—blood and bone!"
At the point of death, Hector, his helmet flashing,
said, "I know you well—I see my fate before me.
Never a chance that I could win you over . . .
Iron inside your chest, that heart of yours.
But now beware, or my curse will draw god's wrath
upon your head, that day when Paris and lord Apollo—
for all your fighting heart—destroy you at the Scaean Gates!"
Death cut him short. The end closed in around him.
Flying free of his limbs
his soul went winging down to the House of Death,
wailing his fate, leaving his manhood far behind,
his young and supple strength. But brilliant Achilles
taunted Hector's body, dead as he was, "Die, die!
For my own death, I'll meet it freely—whenever Zeus
and the other deathless gods would like to bring it on!"

In the face of this unrestrained outburst of rage, in
which Achilles threatens to tear Hector to pieces and
devour the raw flesh himself; and in the face of Hector,
who murmurs his last prophetic words, one might think
that the poem has come to its end. It hasn't. Homer is too
human, Greece too civilized. Achilles tortures the dead
body of his enemy, dragging it behind the chariot to the
grave of Patroclus: but is unable to damage its marble

beauty, which the gods preserve. But, soon afterward, Achilles accepts the ransom that old Priam comes to offer him and even grants an eleven-day truce so that the Trojans can celebrate Hector's funeral. The last, greatest episode of the *Iliad*, in Book XXIV, unexpectedly changes the features of the character Achilles. From pitiless he suddenly becomes compassionate and even kind.

The scene begins at night when Priam, against all advice, decides to cross the plain that separates Troy from the Greek camp to recover the body of his son. The old man is alone in the chariot, but he is soon joined by Hermes, whom Zeus has sent to help him. The god guides Priam to the enemy camp, giving him valuable counsel on how to address Achilles. And unexpectedly Priam enters the tent of the man who has killed so many of his sons, entreats him in the name of his father, Peleus, kisses the hand that murdered Hector. Achilles, who has just finished eating, and is startled at first, weeps, remembering his father and Patroclus; Priam weeps for Hector. "The memory of what is lost brings with it rage and grief," Matteo Nucci writes in his book *The Heroes' Tears*. "The itching nose. And weeping together. Here everyone is weeping. From the poet creator to the reader. But the two men who inspire weeping are these enemies who weep together. And who have overcome every obstacle."[5]

The commonality between men is finally re-established: in weeping. Achilles suddenly gets up, raises the old man by the hand, invites him to sit with him, and launches into a speech on the troubles that the gods force men to live with. Priam refuses to sit as long as Hector lies without burial, and Achilles, always irritable, seems ready to explode. Frightened, Priam sits. Achilles rushes out, along with his men, and has the king's herald enter and unload the immense ransom. Then he calls the handmaidens and has them wash and clothe the body of Hector, and finally he lays him on the bier himself and, breaking into laments for Patroclus, returns to the tent. Then he invites Priam to eat with him, claiming that even Niobe remembered food, though Apollo had killed twelve of her children.

At the end of the meal, the two men, now satisfied, look at and admire each other, in what is the final pause of the poem: Priam notes Achilles' "beauty, his magnificent build—face-to-face he seemed a deathless god"; Achilles observes Priam's "noble looks" and listens to his words.

A great stupor, a profound wonder possesses each man as he looks at the other, as if now, after death, the moment of discovery of the other had arrived, and as if that discovery consisted in the first place in finding beauty again in a human being. Because the *Iliad*, the poem of force and pity, is also the song of beauty.

Before Priam is permitted to go to sleep, Achilles asks him how long a truce will be needed for the funeral celebration. Once in bed, however, the old man is awakened by Hermes, who advises him to depart immediately for Troy with the body of his son. Priam obeys and returns to the city. The rest of Book XXIV is taken up by Hector's funeral, which is summarized in the last line of the poem: "And so the Trojans buried Hector breaker of horses."

Death is necessary so that man can be restored to himself and recognize the beauty of the other. Weeping is necessary so that Priam can also be Peleus and Achilles can for a moment become Hector, so that the hero of force is also the hero of resistance—so that Hector can have the honor of weeping as long as the sun shines on human misery.

II
THE NOVEL OF RETURN: THE *ODYSSEY*

Tell me, Muse, of the man of many ways, who was driven
far journeys, after he had sacked Troy's sacred citadel.
Many were they whose cities he saw, whose minds he learned of,
many the pains he suffered in his spirit on the wide sea,
struggling for his own life and the homecoming of his companions.
Even so he could not save his companions, hard though
he strove to; they were destroyed by their own wild recklessness,
fools, who devoured the oxen of Helios, the Sun God,
and he took away the day of their homecoming. From some point
here, goddess, daughter of Zeus, speak, and begin our story.
Then all the others, as many as fled sheer destruction,
were at home now, having escaped the sea and the fighting.
This only alone, longing for his wife and his homecoming,
was detained by the queenly nymph Kalypso, bright among
    goddesses,
in her hollowed caverns, desiring that he should be her husband.[6]

This is the beginning of the second Homeric poem: the
Odyssey. We don't know, of course, who composed it or
when, exactly: certainly several decades after the *Iliad*. Some
among the ancients maintained that an old Homer had com-
posed it, while the *Iliad* was the work of a young poet. We
can be satisfied with this theory, even if we're aware how
unlikely it is that a young Homer would compose a great

poem like the *Iliad* and then, as an old man, an equally great poem, but completely different, like the *Odyssey*. Today, as I noted in Chapter I, we tend to attribute it to a "second Homer," as mysterious as the second or third Isaiah.

This is because the *Odyssey*, which, as Longinus understood, in many ways "continues" the *Iliad*, and assumes, in any case, that it is known, doesn't talk about war: the *Odyssey* is the poem of return, the poem of the veteran who, after ten years of fighting in Troy, after destroying the city himself, returns home, which takes ten more years. In fact, from the opening lines the poem fits into the more general subject of the difficult *nóstos*, the return of the Greeks to their country after the sack of Troy. The *Odyssey* itself several times evokes the case of Agamemnon, the supreme commander of the Greek army, killed by his wife, Clytemnestra, and her lover Aegisthus as soon as he sets foot in his house. His brother Menelaus, the husband betrayed and abandoned by Helen, reaches his home, in Sparta, after eight years of wandering. Odysseus takes two more, but it should be remembered that the ten years of his *nóstos* include an entire year spent with Circe and seven passed with Calypso: Odysseus therefore spends only two years actually wandering, while he spends eight imprisoned more or less consensually (at least in terms of the seduction) by two powerful and beautiful goddesses.

The *Odyssey* is the poem of return, but it is, above all, a great novel: the first and most enthralling that the Western tradition—and the whole world—knows. It's an epic novel, of course, but still a novel, whose protagonist, Odysseus, is surrounded by a multitude of characters. The women, in the first place: his mother, Anticlea, the old nurse Euryclea, the very young Nausicaa, Circe, Calypso, and, finally, the real co-protagonist, Penelope. The female presence in the poem is extensive and fundamental, more than in any other ancient literary work. Furthermore, the *Odyssey* includes three generations of characters: the oldest generation, represented by Laertes, Odysseus' father, one of the Argonauts (navigation is evidently in the blood of this family), the generation of Odysseus himself and his contemporaries, and that of Telemachus, the son of Odysseus and Penelope. The poem ranges over at least four courts: Ithaca, now occupied and besieged by Penelope's suitors; Pylos, where old Nestor still reigns; Sparta, ruled by Menelaus and Helen; and, finally, the court of the Phaeacians in Scheria, governed by Alcinous and Arete. But the *Odyssey* also has more humble settings: the hut of Eumaeus, the swineherd who offers hospitality to Odysseus when he disembarks on Ithaca; the world of servants and handmaidens who inhabit the palace of Odysseus. And, finally, here, too, is the Olympus of the gods, among whom Poseidon and Athena stand out, the one hostile to Odysseus, the other protective.

Nor can we forget the fantastic places, the exotic lands, that the protagonist visits: situating them around the Mediterranean (with at least a couple of episodes in the Atlantic), as has been done since antiquity, or in Scandinavia, as some scholars today would like to do, is attractive, but in essence unworkable. According to the Greek geographer and philosopher Strabo, when the greatest geographer of antiquity, Eratosthenes, was asked where, precisely, Odysseus had traveled, he answered that if someone could point out the shoemaker who had fabricated the bag of the winds for Aeolus, he would reveal the route of Odysseus' long wandering. Because when the protagonist and his men, coming from Troy (on what is now the northern Mediterranean coast of Turkey, at the entrance to the Dardanelles), reach Cape Maleas, they suffer through a huge storm and then enter an imaginary world: the islands of the Cyclops and of Aeolus, and Circe's Aeaea; Calypso's Ogygia, the Phaeacians' Scheria, Trinachia, with the oxen sacred to the sun, Hades, the land of the Lotus-Eaters, the rocks of the Sirens, the rocks called the Rovers, Scylla and Charybdis—these are all places of the imagination, not reality, even though they may allude to prominent mythic geographies and anthropologies. Not even Ithaca, the center of the poem, seems to be the island we call by that name today.

The geography of the *Odyssey* is as fantastic as the characterization of its protagonist is precise: and it should be noted right away that this is the first literary work that takes its title from the name of the main character, who by his presence, and even by his absence, unifies the entire poem. Odysseus isn't an ordinary protagonist, to judge from his earlier history and from his fortunes in the three thousand years since. He's an ancient, even archaic, hero, but also the prototype of the modern man. A great fighter and among the most respected counselors during the Trojan War, he is the most intelligent of the heroes, the first *Homo sapiens sapiens* of literature: liar and deceiver, he uses his *métis*, his sharp mind, to survive or to obtain the goal he has set for himself: and he always thinks before he speaks or acts. He is also *Homo faber*, who has built with his own hands his marriage bed and the raft that carries him away from Ogygia, the island of Calypso, to Scheria, the land of the Phaeacians.

As the opening lines of the poem say, Odysseus is the hero of knowledge: "Many were they whose cities he saw, whose minds he learned of." Odysseus never stops learning. When his men urge him not to remain in the cave of the Cyclops, the captain answers that he wants to see this monster, and find out if he'll offer him hospitality. Later, although Circe puts him on his guard against the dangers represented by the Sirens, Odysseus wants to listen to them, and for that has himself bound to the main mast, while he plugs up the ears of his companions with wax so that they won't hear the bewitching song.

Yet the Odysseus of the *Odyssey* is still not Dante's, who, driven by "ardor" to have experience of the world, and "of human vices and valor," is unconcerned about returning home, forgets about the love of Penelope, Laertes, and Telemachus in order to cross the unknown ocean: he is not yet a Faust of the sea. He is, rather, the hero of patience, endurance, and survival, one who often says to himself, "Bear up, my heart. You have had worse to endure before this on that day when the irresistible Cyclops ate up my strong companions," and to Calypso he says: "I will endure it, keeping a stubborn spirit inside me, for already I have suffered much and done much hard work on the waves and in the fighting." He's the hero of humanity: a man who refuses immortality, "without old age," which Calypso offers him, along with her divine beauty, in order to return home, to a wife who is old and mortal. Rather, he persistently pursues the fully human happiness of family life: house, wife, father, son—the only that is given on earth.

Odysseus also possesses this primary quality: he's a great talker. We saw it in the *Iliad*, when the old Trojan Antenor recalls his marvelous speeches as an ambassador. In the *Odyssey* this characteristic is repeatedly emphasized, under-scoring the protagonist's powers of intuition, comprehension, and psychological penetration. The most striking example is the speech he makes to Nausicaa, the young daughter of Alcinous, king of the Phaeacians. Since waking up in the morning, the girl has been thinking about her own wedding, and has in effect gone with her handmaidens to the seashore to wash her trousseau, as Athena suggested to her in a dream. Odysseus is naked, encrusted with salt, he looks like a famished lion, "rained on and blown by the wind," who goes out after cattle or sheep, or after wild deer. What to do? Seize Nausicaa by the knees and beg her "in words of blandishment," or speak from a distance? Odysseus stops to think, then he utters a masterpiece of a speech, which praises the girl's beauty in an extraordinary image and seems to read in her eyes her overriding worry:

Then in the division of his heart this way seemed best to him,
to stand well off and supplicate in words of blandishment,
for fear that, if he clasped her knees, the girl might be angry.
So blandishingly and full of craft he began to address her:
"I am at your knees, O queen. But are you mortal or goddess?
If indeed you are one of the gods who hold wide heaven,
then I must find in you the nearest likeness to Artemis

the daughter of great Zeus, for beauty, figure, and stature.
But if you are one among those mortals who live in this country,
three times blessed are your father and the lady your mother,
and three times blessed your brothers too, and I know their spirits
are warmed forever with happiness at the thought of you, seeing
such a slip of beauty taking her place in the chorus of dancers;
but blessed at the heart, even beyond these others, is that one
who, after loading you down with gifts, leads you as his bride
home. I have never with these eyes seen anything like you,
neither man nor woman. Wonder takes me as I look on you.
Yet in Delos once I saw such a thing, by Apollo's altar.
I saw the stalk of a young palm shooting up. I had gone there
once, and with a following of a great many people,
on that journey which was to mean hard suffering for me."

Odysseus is a formidable orator, as he shows in Troy
when he speaks to the soldiers and the leaders of the Greek
army. But now he outdoes himself: first he compares
Nausicaa to Artemis, the virgin of the hunt, the forests, and
the fields; then he proclaims her parents and brothers
blessed when they see that "slip of beauty" begin to dance.
It's here that he inserts his acute, immediate perception of
her mind: blessed beyond all, he says, is the man who will
take her as a bride! Never, he declares, has he seen a mortal
like her: he can compare her only to the "young palm stalk"
that he himself, Odysseus, once saw on Delos. How to
resist such a speech? And how to resist, when Odysseus
washes and Athena showers grace and beauty on his head
and shoulders? Nausicaa doesn't resist: she looks at him in
admiration and to her handmaidens says: "If only the man
to be called my husband could be like this one, a man living
here, if only this one were pleased to stay here."

Ultimately the narrative belongs to Odysseus: when he tells Eumaeus and Penelope and even Athena false stories that seem true; when he describes to Arete, the queen of the Phaeacians, his journey on the sea from Ogygia to Scheria, vividly re-creating the storm that swept away his raft; when, finally, he recounts his own adventures, from Books IX to XII. Because it's Odysseus himself who composes the *Odyssey*, the story of himself. And he does it so well that Alcinous praises the "grace upon your words," and the "sound sense" within them, the expertise of the "aedos." Alcinous would listen to the spellbinding *mýthos* all the long, "endless" night:

"Odysseus, we as we look upon you do not imagine
that you are a deceptive or thievish man, the sort that the black earth
breeds in great numbers, people who wander widely, making up
lying stories, from which no one could learn anything. You have
a grace upon your words, and there is sound sense within them,
and expertly, as a singer would do, you have told the story
of the dismal sorrows befallen yourself and all of the Argives.
But come now, tell me this and give me an accurate answer:
Did you see any of your godlike companions, who once with you
went to Ilion and there met their destiny? Here is
a night that is very long, it is endless. It is not time yet
to sleep in the palace. But go on telling your wonderful story.
I myself could hold out until the bright dawn,
if only you could bear to tell me, here in the palace, of your
sufferings."

Odysseus is all this and more: he is, therefore, *polýtropos*, a man of many sides and many places, and *polýmetis*, with many minds and many skills, with many plots, with a multifarious character. This is why, in essence, he exerts a fascination that has endured up to our time.

The structure of the poem is as complex as the character of Odysseus. The *Iliad* is "simple in construction and closer to tragedy," says Aristotle in the *Poetics*, and the *Odyssey* "complex and closer to comedy," because of the recognitions, the "characters," the surprises. The structure consists essentially of four blocks: Books I–IV, V–VIII, IX–XII, and XIII–XXIV. In the first, called the Telemachy, Odysseus isn't even present, although he's in the thoughts of everyone who is present. The narrative follows the situation in Ithaca, with the suitors besieging the queen and occupying the palace, while Telemachus tries to rebel. Telemachus goes to Pylos and Sparta, seeking news of his father from Nestor and Menelaus.

The protagonist arrives in Book V, and remains till the end. In Book V Hermes flies from Olympus to Ogygia to inform Calypso that the gods have decided that she has to allow her lover-prisoner to depart. Odysseus constructs his raft and sets sail for Ithaca. He has spent seven years with the goddess, which he will later call "terrible": the daughter of Atlas, the Titan who supports the world on his shoulders. But there is nothing terrible about Calypso, who wants simply to "hide" him (that is the etymology of her name), to conceal him on her island, on the margins of the world, remove him from time with her love, give him immortality without old age. Calypso rescued Odysseus when—dragged by the sea for nine days, after passing between Scylla and Charybdis, and losing all his companions—he was tossed onto her island, Ogygia. The years she spends with Odysseus, who gives her some earthly happiness, transform Calypso into a caring woman, into a companion who not only helps but even collaborates, with active affection, in outfitting the raft.

In reality the episode of Calypso, although short in terms of the story, marks a turning point in the events of the poem. Framed by two tremendous storms, the one that carries Odysseus to Ogygia and the one that almost causes him to perish when he leaves, it constitutes the pause, the interlude that removes him from the world and worldly adventures, and subjects him to the insidious distraction and temptation of immortality, of becoming a god, so that he may be restored to life and to manhood: a condition that he fully regains when he lands, truly No One now, on the Phaeacians' shore. There Odysseus returns.

Leaving Calypso, Odysseus sets sail for Ithaca. Poseidon sees him on the sea and stirs up a terrifying storm: the boat shatters, the sailor ends up in the midst of gigantic waves, and is saved only by the intervention of the nymph Ino and then by his capacity to reflect and his skill in swimming. The description of this storm in two acts, re-evoked and summarized later by Odysseus himself for the queen of the Phaeacians, Arete, is one of four (in Books V, VII, IX, and XII) that made the *Odyssey* famous in antiquity and that still make it memorable: one of the few features of the second Homeric poem that Longinus judged sublime.

The mixture of sound, repetition, and similes is extraordinary. Poseidon unleashes the winds, which, rushing at one another, "rolled up a heavy sea." Odysseus despairs and regrets that he didn't die in Troy, but an immense wave hits him, throws him off the raft, breaks the mast, sinks him. Returning to the surface, he grabs the boat again and sits in the middle, but the winds carry him here and there "as the North Wind in autumn tumbles and tosses thistle-down along the plain, and the bunches hold fast one on another." The nymph Ino sees him and offers him her great veil. Suspicious, Odysseus decides to stick to the raft as long as it holds together, but Poseidon immediately rouses another wave, "terrible and rough, and it curled over and broke down," and scatters the wood everywhere "as when the wind blows hard on a dry pile of chaff, and scatters it abroad in every direction." Odysseus strips and starts swimming. Poseidon curses him, but Athena intervenes, calming the winds. Odysseus is driven over the sea for two days, and on the third he spies land nearby and is filled with longing to reach it, "as welcome as the show of life again in a father is to his children, when he has lain sick, suffering strong pains, and wasting long away, and the hateful death spirit has brushed him, but then, and it is welcome, the gods set him free of his sickness."

While Odysseus swims even more vigorously toward the land, he hears a powerful wave roaring against the coast. It seems to him that there is no escape now. At the very moment he gives voice to anguish, a great surge drives him onto the rocky coast. He grabs the rock with his bare hands and holds on until the great wave passes: flowing out, however, it strikes him straight on and throws him again into the open sea: "As when an octopus is dragged away from its shelter the thickly-clustered pebbles stick in the cups of the tentacles, so in contact with the rock the skin from his bold hands was torn away. Now the great sea covered him over."

Finally, after this incredible test of endurance—for the protagonist and also for the poet—Odysseus comes ashore in the land of the Phaeacians and collapses in the bushes near the bank of a river. He falls asleep; he is awakened by the cries of Nausicaa, the daughter of Alcinous, and her handmaidens, and she helps him get to the palace. The scene remains in the royal palace and its marvelous gardens, with banquets, the bard Demodocus' songs, and athletic games, until the end of Book VIII, when Alcinous asks his guest who he is.

At the start of Book IX Odysseus reveals his identity and then begins to narrate his own adventures: these—the so-called Apologue of Alcinous—include the Ciconians, the Lotus-Eaters, Cyclops, Aeolus, Laistrygones, Circe, Hades, the Sirens, Scylla and Charybdis, the Island of the Sun, and Calypso, and continue to the end of Book XII. This is the long flashback of the *Odyssey*, which is the first tale to use a technique that has had huge success in Western fiction (and cinema).

With Book XIII Odysseus, transported by a Phaeacian ship, finally reaches Ithaca, where he is left, asleep, and he doesn't recognize it until Athena, taking the form of a boy, shows it to him. Odysseus and the goddess hide the treasure that the Phaeacians have given him, then Athena disguises him as an old beggar and the hero goes to Eumaeus' hut. There, in Book XVI, Odysseus reveals himself to Telemachus, who has just returned from his journey to Pylos and Sparta, escaping a trap set by the suitors on his way home. Thus begins the slow, laborious reconquest of house and wife that the hero must accomplish. Preceded by Telemachus, Odysseus and Eumaeus reach the palace, in Book XVII: the first encounter is with the dog Argos, who after twenty years recognizes in the approaching beggar his master, Odysseus, and dies immediately afterward. Two other key encounters take place in Book XIX, when Penelope receives the new beggar but doesn't recognize him, even though she's present at the moment when Euryclea, washing his legs, discovers the scar from the wound inflicted by a wild boar when he went hunting as a boy on Mt. Parnassus. Penelope, however, tells the beggar the trick she has perpetrated on the suitors with the shroud for Laertes, woven by day and undone at night, and then her intention of proposing to the suitors the contest of the bow. Whoever succeeds in stringing Odysseus' old bow and shooting the arrow through the axe heads will have her as his wife.

The contest takes place in Book XXI, with Telemachus in the lists: he is about to succeed (if he wins, his mother will remain with him), but Odysseus signals him to stop. Then Antinous, the first of the suitors, tries, but he fails miserably. After him, Eurymachus. Odysseus goes out and, by means of the scar on his thigh, reveals to Eumaeus and Philoitios who he is. Returning, he asks to try the bow, which finally is handed to him, while Penelope is sent to her rooms by Telemachus. The doors of the hall are closed by Euryclea, the old beggar turns the weapon over in his hands, tests its strength, then strings it as if it were a lyre, cocks an arrow, and shoots it so that it passes through all the axes. When Book XXII opens, Odysseus strips off his rags, jumps onto the threshold, and aims an arrow at the throat of Antinous, piercing him. The suitors shout and insult him, believing he hit him by mistake. "Looking darkly upon them," Odysseus raises a furious shout of vengeance and war:

"You dogs, you never thought that I would any more come back
from the land of Troy, and because of that you despoiled my house-
  hold,
and forcibly took my serving women to sleep beside you,
and sought to win my wife while I was still alive, fearing
neither the immortal gods who hold the wide heaven,
nor any resentment sprung from men to be yours in the future.
Now upon all of you the terms of destruction are fastened."

With these words begins Odysseus' revenge, a true massacre that spares no one except the bard Phemius. The suitors are exterminated without pity; for a while Odysseus becomes again the fierce warrior of Troy.

Book XXIII is devoted entirely to the recognition and the reunion between Odysseus and Penelope, the event that all listeners to and readers of the poem have been waiting for from the beginning. When the slaughter is over, old Euryclea hurries up the stairs to Penelope, in the marriage bed, and finds her asleep. She wakes her, announcing that her husband has returned. Penelope thinks she's mad and reproaches her harshly. But the nurse insists: it really is Odysseus, he is the stranger they all insulted, the old beggar. Penelope rejoices, jumps out of bed, embraces the old woman, weeps, asks her what happened. Euryclea answers that she didn't see it nor has she been told: she only heard the cries of those who were killed. Then she asks Penelope to come down with her, to be reunited with her husband. But Penelope, prudent, attributes the slaughter to a god, maintaining that Odysseus was lost far from home. Then the old woman tells her about the scar. And finally Penelope decides to go down, to find her son, to see the dead suitors "and the man who killed them."

The scene that follows is one of the literary master-pieces of all time. When she enters the hall, the woman is uncertain whether to question her husband from a distance or go to him and "kiss his head and hands." She sits opposite Odysseus, in the firelight, while he, looking down, sits leaning against a pillar, waiting for her to speak. Penelope, however, is silent, while, in a stupor, she looks at him: at times she recognizes him, at others, instead, looking at the rags he's wearing, she doesn't. Telemachus reproaches her: why do you stay far from my father, why don't you sit next to him? You have a heart harder than a stone. No other woman would stay like that, "with spirit as stubborn as yours," far from a husband who returns after twenty years. She answers, however, that if that really is Odysseus, well, they have secret signs that will allow them to recognize each other. Odysseus smiles and speaks to his son: let your mother test me, I'm dirty now and wearing these wretched clothes, and so she doesn't know me. But we need to think of the reactions of the suitors' families. Telemachus lets his father, wiser and more experienced, take care of that, and Odysseus suggests that they all have a bath and put on tunics: the singer, then, will lead a dance such that the passersby, outside, will think that they are celebrating a wedding at the palace. The steward, Eurynome, bathes him. Athena, as usual, pours "great beauty" over his head and he comes out of the bath "looking like an immortal," and immediately sits down in the place he had left.

Yet again Penelope doesn't move. Now Odysseus reproaches her: no other woman, he repeats, using the same words as Telemachus, would be like that, "with spirit as stubborn as yours, would keep back" from a husband who returns after twenty years. So he orders the old nurse, Euryclea, to prepare him a bed here in the hall, so he can sleep, even alone: "she has a heart of iron within her." Then, finally, Penelope speaks: yes, make the bed, bring out the bed from the marriage chamber, and lie on the bed, here in the hall. "What you have said, dear lady, has hurt my heart deeply," Odysseus interrupts her. No one could move my bed: I built it myself from an olive tree that grew in the grounds. It's rooted in the earth. Odysseus lingers at length on the way he built and decorated the marriage bed. Finally, Penelope can't resist anymore, her knees and heart melt, because she has recognized the secret signs her husband has offered her. Weeping, she runs to him, throws her arms around his neck, kisses his head and says to him:

"Do not be angry with me, Odysseus, since, beyond other men,
you have the most understanding. The gods
granted us misery, in jealousy over the thought that we two, always
    together,
should enjoy our youth, and then come to the threshold of old age.
Then do not now be angry with me nor blame me, because

I did not greet you, as I do now, at first when I saw you.
For always the spirit deep in my very heart was fearful
that some one of mortal men would come my way and deceive me
with words. For there are many who scheme for wicked advantage.
For neither would the daughter born to Zeus, Helen of Argos,
have lain in love with an outlander from another country,
if she had known that the warlike sons of the Achaians would bring
    her
home again to the beloved land of her fathers.
It was a god who stirred her to do the shameful thing she
did, and never before had she had in her heart this terrible
wildness, out of which came suffering to us also.
But now, since you have given me accurate proof describing
our bed, which no other mortal man beside has ever seen,
but only you and I, and there is one serving woman,
Aktor's daughter, whom my father gave me when I came here,
who used to guard the doors for us in our well-built chamber;
so you persuade my heart, though it has been very stubborn."

Weeping, the two then set out for that bed which Penelope has used as the supreme test of Odysseus' identity. She has him tell her his adventures, and he adds the prophecy of Tiresias. Athena restrains the horses of Aurora, prolonging the night of love regained.

But the poem isn't over yet: if the suitors and faithless handmaidens have been eliminated, their relatives still have to be held off, while their souls, guided by Hermes, descend to Hades and meet Agamemnon, to whom they tell their tale. Odysseus, meanwhile, goes to the countryside to see his father. Yet another moving scene of recognition takes place. Then the two arm themselves for the fight with the victims' relatives. But Athena stops both sides and imposes peace.

The *Odyssey* is therefore a *romance* with a finale that for a moment is in danger of turning tragic. It is full of ordeals, disasters, shipwrecks, marvels, monsters, and enchantresses, and populated by grand old men, extremely grand old women, and the most adorable girl who ever appeared in a story, Nausicaa. In the *Odyssey*, there is the Old Man of the Sea—Proteus who can change into a thousand shapes—and the one-eyed Cyclops, tranquil shepherd and cheese maker, but also, if necessary, a fierce cannibal of uncooked Greeks and drunken drinker of unwatered Greek wine. Miraculous objects appear: the gentle lotus flower that makes one forget everything, even the strongest affections, and the plant *moly* that is protection against spells; a leather bag that contains all the winds and a veil that calms the waves.

The *Odyssey* is a sequel to the *Iliad* (its "epilogue," says the author of *On the Sublime*), taking up episodes and images from it and adding details that the first Homer didn't care to recount: Odysseus as a spy inside Troy, recognized by Helen alone, the quarrel between Odysseus and Achilles, even the taking of the city. In the *Odyssey*, the second Homer has the protagonist speak to his former companions, now dead: Agamemnon, Achilles, Ajax. He has him meet his dead mother.

These conversations in Hades open up the world of death to the protagonist and to readers: it's the first view in Western poetry. Odysseus, meeting Anticlea, his mother, is frustrated three times in his attempt to embrace her, so that the son asks why she doesn't wait when he is trying to hold her, or if Persephone has sent him a ghost. No, Anticlea answers:

"This is not Persephone, daughter of Zeus, beguiling you,
but it is only what happens, when they die, to all mortals.
The sinews no longer hold the flesh and the bones together,
and once the spirit has left the white bones, all the rest
of the body is made subject to the fire's strong fury,
but the soul flitters out like a dream and flies away."

To learn what dying means, and learn it from the lips of one's own mother, and discover that she died of longing for her son, is something that for a few instants freezes the blood. Anticlea urges Odysseus to turn back quickly toward the light, return swiftly to life, but he starts talking to Agamemnon and Achilles, who are also dead. And if the first speaks only of the betrayal of his wife, Clytemnestra, and of how she and Aegisthus killed him on his return from Troy, "like an ox at his manger," Achilles, before the praise of his old companion, yet again confirms the meaning of death:

"O shining Odysseus, never try to console me for dying.
I would rather follow the plow as thrall to another
man, one with no land allotted him and not much to live on,
than be a king over all the perished dead."

Certainly both Agamemnon and Achilles demonstrate a very strong attachment to the world of the living, the former asking about Orestes, the latter about his son Neoptolemus and his father, Peleus, but what they reveal about the "being of having been," as Walter Otto called it, is much more frightening. When Odysseus and his companions return to Circe after the visit to Hades, the goddess welcomes them with a special greeting: "Unhappy men, who went alive to the house of Hades, so dying twice, when all the rest of mankind die only once."

In contrast to that experience of horror, the *Odyssey* touches the feelings of Nausicaa with infinite delicacy. Nausicaa, we have seen, admires Odysseus with amazement, after he has washed and dressed, and hopes that "a man like that" can become her husband. Later, after he's had another bath, she says goodbye to him for the last time:

Nausikaa, with the gods' loveliness on her,
stood beside the pillar that supported the roof with its joinery,
and gazed upon Odysseus with all her eyes and admired him,
and spoke to him aloud and addressed him in winged words, saying:
"Goodbye, stranger, and think of me sometimes when you are
back at home, how I was the first you owed your life to."
Then resourceful Odysseus spoke in turn and answered her:
"Nausikaa, daughter of great-hearted Alkinoös,
even so may Zeus, high-thundering husband of Hera,
grant me to reach my house and see my day of homecoming.
So even when I am there I will pray to you, as to a goddess,
all the days of my life. For, maiden, my life was your gift."

And yet Nausicaa's tender feeling, on which the second Homer never lingers romantically, finds accents of bourgeois comedy when Alcinous, her father, in conversation with Odysseus, reproaches his daughter for not having brought him to the city in the chariot with her, and then declares that he would have been very happy to keep him as a son-in-law, here on Scheria.

Comedy does have a place in the poem, and not only the comedy of manners that Longinus saw in it but the low comedy of the fight between the two beggars, Irus and Odysseus, in front of the palace on Ithaca; the higher comedy, mixed with terror, of Polyphemus drunk; and the highest, almost, in truth, sublime comedy that marks the love of Ares and Aphrodite, as the bard of the Phaeacians, the blind Demodocus, sings it. The truly "Homeric" laughter that all the gods break into after seeing Ares and Aphrodite trapped, naked, in the invisible net of the cuckolded Hephaestus, and the little scene where Apollo asks Hermes if he wouldn't like to go to bed with Aphrodite, and he responds, "I wish it could only be, and there could be thrice this number of endless fastenings," are pure entertainment and fun.

In contrast to this comic verve there is the most moving pathos, as in the episode of Argos, in Book XVII. Argos lies on a pile of dung at the entrance to the palace. When he sees Odysseus he wags his tail and pricks his ears, but hasn't the strength to approach his old master, who, after twenty years, is nearby. Odysseus, in fact, looks away and wipes a tear, "without Eumaeus noticing"; Eumaeus, who accompanies him, is still unaware of the identity of the beggar with whom he is about to enter the palace. But the beggar knows how to distract the swineherd, praising the animal ("Amazing, this dog that lies on the dunghill. The shape of him is splendid!") and, right afterward, expressing the doubt that, rather than a hunting dog, he might have been a "table dog," that gentlemen keep "for show." Eumaeus replies yes, "this is the dog of a man who perished far away," but no, he wasn't a table dog: he was a swift hunter and knew how to follow the game "in the profound depths of the forest." Now, instead, he is wretched, because, with his master dead, the women don't look after him.

As soon as he's spoken these words, Eumaeus enters the house, heading toward the hall. "But the doom of dark death now closed over the dog, Argos," the second Homer concludes, "when, after nineteen years had gone by, he had seen Odysseus." Argos, unlike Euryclea, Penelope, and Laertes, has no need of proofs to recognize his master, even if he is disguised as a poor beggar. The dog immediately knows Odysseus, even twenty years later, but for him recognition means dying. Homer doesn't say if the animal dies of pure emotion, or if his heart, like the Duke of Gloucester's in *King Lear*, "burst smilingly." The reader is invited to make his choice, but the impression we get from the coincidence between recognition and death is that, if Argos could speak, he would exclaim, with Simeon in the Gospel of Luke: "Lord, now lettest thou thy servant depart in peace, according to thy word: For mine eyes have seen thy salvation."

The episode of Argos is only one in the emotional structure of the poem, which also includes Odysseus' encounters with his mother, Anticlea, in Hades, and his father, Laertes, in his vineyard.

Laertes, who completes the restoration of the family, thanks to the scar and certain objects—the pear trees, apple trees, fig trees of the farm—as simple as Penelope's bed, brings the *Odyssey* to a close in the name of the father: like the *Iliad* with the scene of Priam and Achilles, in which a father entreats in the name of the father.

In fact the *Odyssey* is constructed in a particular

tonality, in which pathos alternates with the fantastic. No one understood this better than Longinus, who sees the young Homer of the *Iliad* as a strong, agonistic poet, vibrating with dramatic tension, the old man of the *Odyssey* as a poet dedicated to fables. He doesn't spare his criticisms of the second Homer, in particular for what he calls the "frivolity" of certain episodes, like the leather bag of the winds, the men transformed into swine by Circe, Zeus "nurtured by the doves like a nestling." A ship-wrecked man who goes ten days without touching food, or the "incredible story" of the killing of the suitors, he writes, are really "dreams of Zeus." Naturally such judgments could be examined more closely, but the fact remains that the author who pronounces them has also analyzed the *Odyssey* with singular insight:

Thus, in the *Odyssey*, Homer may be likened to the setting sun: the grandeur remains but without the intensity; for no longer there does he maintain the same pitch as in those lays of Troy. There is not the consistent level of sublimity which nowhere lapses into mediocrity, nor is there the same closely packed profusion of passions, nor the versatility and realism studded with images drawn from real life. As though the ocean were withdrawing into itself and remaining quietly within its own bounds, from now on we see the ebbing of Homer's greatness as he wanders in the realms of the fabulous and the incredible. In saying this I have not forgotten the storms in the *Odyssey* and the episode of the Cyclops and other things of the kind. I am speaking of old age, but it is, after all, the old age of Homer. Nevertheless, in every one of these passages the fabulous predominates over the real.

The *Odyssey*, however, goes well beyond the criticisms and the praise of Longinus. For example, it develops a discourse on poetics and has a theological design very different from that of the *Iliad*. As for its poetics, there are three narrators in the poem, the two bards and Odysseus himself. When, in Book I, the bard of Ithaca, Phemius, starts describing the "sad return" of the Greeks from Troy, Penelope, who has just come down from her rooms to the suitors, bursts into tears, reproaching Phemius, who knows so many subjects that "charm men's hearts," yet chooses that, in front of her, who is always remembering, always yearning for her husband, lost on his return. Telemachus interrupts her, proclaiming at the same time a poetics of the new and a theological vision:

"Why, my mother, do you begrudge this excellent singer
his pleasing himself as the thought drives him? It is not the singers
who are to blame, it must be Zeus is to blame, who gives out
to men who eat bread, to each and all, the way he wills it.
There is nothing wrong in his singing the sad return of the Danaans.
People, surely, always give more applause to that song
which is the latest to circulate among the listeners."

The Phaeacians, too, share this poetics of the new: they not only listen with evident pleasure to the songs of Demodocus about the Trojan War but are enchanted, as we've seen, by Odysseus' long story of his own adventures, which, for Alcinous, makes him like a bard. Besides, what Alcinous says to Odysseus in Book IX is similar to what Odysseus himself says in speaking of Demodocus in Book VIII, and to what Eumaeus says when, in Book XVII, he tells Penelope about the fascination of the old beggar's tales: "But as when a man looks to a singer, who has been given from the gods the skill with which he sings for delight of mortals, and they are impassioned and strain to hear it when he sings to them, so he enchanted me in the halls as he sat beside me."

The key word in all these contexts is *thélgein*: enchant, bewitch. With his stories, Odysseus enchants, bewitches, even more than a bard. The same verb is used by Circe when she warns Odysseus about the Sirens' song:

"You will come first of all to the Sirens, who are enchanters
of all mankind and whoever comes their way; and that man
who unsuspecting approaches them, and listens to the Sirens
singing, has no prospect of coming home and delighting
his wife and little children as they stand about him in greeting,
but the Sirens by the melody of their singing enchant him.
They sit in their meadow, but the beach before it is piled with boneheaps
of men now rotted away, and the skins shrivel upon them."

The Sirens enchant, Circe says twice, and right away she establishes a mysterious, disturbing, and meaningful bond between their song and death. Warned, Odysseus will escape the darkest fate by having himself tied to the main mast and plugging his companions' ears with wax so that they won't hear the song. Yet he doesn't escape the enchantment of the Sirens: he listens to their entire song and begs to be released from the ropes so he can fling himself at them.

Odysseus can't feel any erotic attraction to the Sirens, since, in portrayals of the time, they are represented not as the seductive girls of future centuries but as two evil birds with female faces, equipped with sharp beaks and prominent claws. Something different, besides the ineffable sweetness of the song, must come into play. Cicero approaches the mystery when, in *De finibus bonorum et malorum* (*On the Ends of Good and Evil*) he reads the Sirens as *cupiditas sapientiae*, passion for learning: Homer, Cicero writes, after translating the relevant lines of *Odyssey* XXI, realized that his story wouldn't seem plausible if a man as great as Odysseus had been held, enmeshed, merely by "alluring strains" ("*si cantiunculis tantus irretitus vir teneretur*"): "It is knowledge that the Sirens offer, and it was no marvel if a lover of wisdom held this dearer than his home."[7] In fact, it seems precisely that which the Sirens of the *Odyssey* sing to Odysseus when, in a "calm without a breath of wind," a divinity puts the waves to sleep and the enchantresses finally appear:

"Come this way, honored Odysseus, great glory of the Achaians,
and stay your ship, so that you can listen here to our singing;
for no one else has ever sailed past this place in his black ship
until he has listened to the honey-sweet voice that issues
from our lips; then goes on, well pleased, knowing more than ever
he did; for we know everything that the Argives and Trojans
did and suffered in wide Troy through the gods' despite.
Over all the generous earth we know everything that happens."

The Sirens thus resemble the Muses, who, as the poet says in Book II of the *Iliad*, "know everything": they know the past of the Trojan War (but who, after the *Iliad*, didn't?), and possess a sort of omniscience regarding present events. The second Homer doesn't tell us what the Sirens know, or what they sing to Odysseus, apart from their omniscience.

Italo Calvino, for example, thought that it was the Sirens themselves who sang the *Odyssey*.

The second Homeric poem, which for Calvino contains numerous odysseys, is therefore full of enchantment, of *thélgein*. Might the poetics of the *Odyssey* as such consist precisely of this, of en-chanting? The figure of the blind bard, Demodocus, has undeniably contributed to the formation of the iconic Homer. And Demodocus, like Homer, sings stories from the Trojan epic. Odysseus later narrates the *Odyssey* itself, or the fabulist, marvelous, and incantatory nucleus of the poem. In short, it seems evident that the *Odyssey*, the supreme example of the "new" song, wants to amaze, enchant, bewitch.

We've seen how Telemachus ties together poetics and theology in his brief speech to his mother in Book I, blaming Zeus for the Greeks' "sad return."

But first, right at the start of the poem, a council of the gods is held, without Poseidon, Odysseus' enemy, who has gone to see the Ethiopians for a hecatomb and the related feast. The council is opened by Zeus, who definitively rejects the charge that men frequently address to the gods (we've seen it in the *Iliad*) that they are the cause of human evils:

"Oh for shame, how the mortals put the blame upon us
gods, for they say evils come from us, but it is they, rather,
who by their own recklessness win sorrow beyond what is given,
as now lately, beyond what was given, Aigisthos
married the wife of Atreus' son, and murdered him on his
    homecoming,
though he knew it was sheer destruction, for we ourselves had told him,

sending Hermes, the mighty watcher, Argeïphontes,
not to kill the man, nor court his lady for marriage."

The gods had warned Aegisthus, with "kind intention":
beware, Orestes will exact revenge for Agamemnon.
Aegisthus went his own way instead. It's not quite the prin-
ciple of free will, not yet: but it's a first move in that direc-
tion, and a move that has some justifying reflection in the
revenge that Odysseus takes on the suitors, who have been
warned, in an oblique manner, by the apocalyptic prophecy
that Theoclymenus utters in Book XX. Fate, so omnipotent
in the *Iliad*, seems to have a minor role in the *Odyssey*, and
even the clashes between the gods are limited to the feud
between Poseidon and Athena.

The theological problems of the *Odyssey* are different.
For example, the killing of the cattle of the Sun is so impor-
tant that it is evoked at the very beginning of the poem and
again, later, in the prophecy of Tiresias. Fate leaves the
companions of Odysseus free to respect them or not, but
the gods cause hunger and storms and sudden sleep, so
that only the second possibility is fulfilled, that is, the com-
panions of Odysseus kill the cows: free will, then, moves on
the razor's edge. Logically, the same holds true for the
blinding of Polyphemos: should Odysseus have let himself
be devoured by the Cyclops to avoid the anger of
Poseidon, his father? And again: Poseidon, in agreement
with Zeus, turns to stone the ship in which the Phaeacians
have brought Odysseus back to Ithaca. Well, Zeus, the
Italian author Pietro Citati writes, in his book on Odysseus
and the *Odyssey*, "performs an action against justice,

because he sacrifices the Phaeacians, who are defenders of hospitality, which is dear and precious to him."[8] Poseidon would like to crush the entire city of the Phaeacians under a rock: if Zeus agrees, he sacrifices a just people to the sea god's revenge; if he listens to the supplications of the Phaeacians, "he is restored to his glory as the god of justice." The *Odyssey*, in one of its formidable omissions, *doesn't* say what in fact happened, and so its readers will never know "if our world is governed by a god of revenge or a god of justice." No theodicy can naturally be founded on such a fragile basis.

There is a further aspect of the *Odyssey* that we don't very often reflect on. The poem appears both closed and open. It concludes formally with the peace imposed by Athena on the two factions who are about to confront each other in battle: Odysseus and his men on one side, the relatives of the suitors killed by Odysseus on the other. But it remains open because the prophecy that Tiresias makes to Odysseus when he visits Hades, and which Odysseus then repeats word for word to Penelope, foresees not only the hero's return home but also a final journey and then death:

"You may punish the violences of these men, when you come home.
But after you have killed these suitors in your own palace,
either by treachery, or openly with the sharp bronze,
then you must take up your well-shaped oar and go on a journey
until you come where there are men living who know nothing
of the sea, and who eat food that is not mixed with salt, who never
have known ships whose cheeks are painted purple, who never

have known well-shaped oars, which act for ships as wings do.
And I will tell you a very clear proof, and you cannot miss it.
When, as you walk, some other wayfarer happens to meet you,
and says you carry a winnow-fan on your bright shoulder,
then you must plant your well-shaped oar in the ground, and render
ceremonious sacrifice to the lord Poseidon,
one ram and one bull, and a mounter of sows, a boar pig,
and make your way home again and render holy hecatombs
to the immortal gods who hold the wide heaven, all
of them in order. Death will come to you from the sea, in
some altogether unwarlike way, and it will end you
in the ebbing time of a sleek old age. Your people
about you will be prosperous. All this is true that I tell you."

The prophecy of Tiresias is ambiguous, in the first place regarding the final journey, which is to take Odysseus, carrying an oar over his shoulder, to a land whose inhabitants do not know oars, ships, food mixed with salt. We wonder what land the second Homer could have in mind, as a poet who is clearly the exponent of a civilization that is based on the sea, and in which all, naturally, know salt, oars, and ships. The second Homer would have had to imagine a land so far interior—Kazakhstan, Congo, Austria, Switzerland—and so far from the sea as to be ignorant of it. The prospect is so unlikely, in the context of ancient Greece, that we might think the text suggests a journey that lasts forever, a journey without end.

In the following millennia some commentators have, in effect, understood it that way, with Odysseus making a final journey that extends infinitely in space and time. In the fourteenth century, Dante, who didn't know Homer but had in all probability read summaries of the *Odyssey* and allusions to it, sends Odysseus into the open sea, and has him pass the Pillars of Hercules and head south and west in the Atlantic until he reaches the mountain of Purgatory, which Dante places at the antipodes of Jerusalem. After him, many—including historians, poets, and explorers of the Renaissance and, in the nineteenth century, Tennyson—have taken Inferno XXVI to suggest that Odysseus discovered America: not an infinite journey but certainly one that is enormously amplified in space and time.

The other anomaly of Tiresias' prophecy lies in the vision he offers of Odysseus' death. According to the Theban prophet, Odysseus will return from the final journey (which rules out that it can be without end). Then, however, Tiresias declares that death, which will take the hero "in some altogether unwarlike way . . . and in the ebbing time of a sleek old age," and surrounded by "prosperous" people, will come to him *ex halós*, from the sea. The *ex* of the original, however, could mean that death will come to Odysseus "from out of the sea"—for example, by means of a sea monster, or someone who arrives by sea, or even a shipwreck—or it might, in accord with the last lines, mean dying "far from the sea," of a sleek old age and surrounded by happy people in his own land.

This ambiguity, too, has opened numerous paths both to interpreters and to narrators and poets: for example, in the *Telegony*, apparently composed by Eugammon, Odysseus is killed by Telegonus, the son he had with Circe in the year they spend together. Telegonus, sent by Circe in search of his father, is cast onto Ithaca by a storm; not knowing where he is, he raids the livestock of Odysseus, who rushes to defend his property. The two fight, and Telegonus, unaware of who he is, kills his father with his spear, whose tip is the poisonous stinger of a devilfish. Thus a thing that has come "from the sea" kills the hero. In the original version of Eliot's *The Waste Land*, on the other hand, the sailor who will later receive the name of Phlebas the Phoenician and who, from the beginning of Section IV of the poem, is an Odysseus (he has "much seen and much endured," Eliot writes, following the third and fourth lines of the *Odyssey*) who undergoes "death by water," that is, a shipwreck, which takes up the death of the Dantean Odysseus cited at the end of the episode.

Thus the *Odyssey* is closed and open at the same time. But it concludes definitively with some lines in Book XXIII. When Penelope, after recognizing Odysseus by his revealing answer to her question about moving their bed, runs to him, embraces him, and kisses his head, he holds her close to him, weeping. Then the second Homer launches into a simile:

She spoke, and still more roused in him the passion for weeping.
He wept as he held his lovely wife, whose thoughts were virtuous.
And as when the land appears welcome to men who are swimming,
after Poseidon has smashed their strong-built ship on the open
water, pounding it with the weight of wind and the heavy seas,
and only a few escape the gray water landward
by swimming, with a thick scurf of salt coated upon them,
and gladly they set foot on the shore, escaping the evil;
so welcome was her husband to her as she looked upon him,
and she could not let him go from the embrace of her white arms.

This is a truly marvelous simile, because it begins with Odysseus: "roused in *him* the passion for weeping. He wept as he held his lovely wife." The images of the simile confirm that it's him. The story of the poem sees him escape shipwreck many times, and at least once the poet paints him encrusted with salt. Yes, it's Odysseus and this is his poem. But the penultimate line of the passage declares that the simile should be applied to her, to Penelope: "so welcome was her husband to her as she looked upon him." It's Penelope who, already pounded by the wind and the harsh waves, with the ship smashed, has survived the shipwreck, and whose body is now crusted with salt. Penelope, too, has escaped a shipwreck and touches the land gladly.

Penelope is like Odysseus, *is* Odysseus, and Odysseus is Penelope: both have suffered the *Odyssey* and become again a single thing when the poem approaches its conclusion. They are the seal of the *Odyssey*: the happiness that closes and encloses. With them, after so much sea, we touch the land *gladly*.

III
THE BIRTH OF THOUGHT: MYTH AND POETRY

From the muses of Helicon let us begin our singing, that haunt
Helicon's great and holy mountain and dance on their soft feet round
the violet-dark spring and the altar of the mighty son of Kronos. And
when they have bathed their gentle skin in Permessos, or the Horse's
Fountain, or holy Olmeios, then on the highest slope of Helicon they
make their dances, fair and lovely, stepping lively in time.[9]

Thus opens Hesiod's *Theogony*. We're in the eighth cen-
tury B.C., and the *Theogony* marks a fundamental moment
in the development of Greek culture and poetry. Certainly
closer chronologically to the *Odyssey* than to the *Iliad*, it
inaugurates a type of poetry very different from both:
poetry that describes the Beginning, the first day of the
world. It's neither the poem of force and pity, like the *Iliad*,
nor, like the *Odyssey*, the poem of return, with its travails
and happiness, but the poem of the creation of the cosmos,
the mythical search for first causes. It corresponds not to
the Homeric poems but to the first chapter of Genesis in
the Bible or its parallels in Sumero-Babylonian and
Egyptian cultures.

The *Theogony* is a central text because it recounts, as the
title itself says, the genesis of the gods, but also because
from the start it establishes an implicit parallel between the

beginning of the universe and the beginning of song, of poetry. It's the Muses who, "veiled in thick mist," first go into the night, "uttering beautiful voice" and celebrating the gods. More explicitly and more fully than in Homer, they inspire Hesiod:

And once they taught Hesiod fine singing, as he tended his lambs below holy Helicon. This is what the goddesses said to me first, the Olympian Muses, daughters of Zeus the aegis-bearer:

"Shepherds that camp in the wild, disgraces, merest bellies:
we know to tell many lies that sound like truth,
but we know to sing reality when we will."

So said mighty Zeus' daughters, the sure of utterance, and they gave me a branch of springing bay to pluck for a staff, a handsome one, and they breathed into me wondrous voice, so that I should celebrate things of the future and things that were aforetime. And they told me to sing of the family of blessed ones who are for ever, and first and last always to sing of themselves.

The Muses, daughters of Zeus, instruct the shepherd poet to sing "reality," not the "many lies that sound like truth" that are Homer's subject. Hesiod is like the shepherd of Book VIII of the *Iliad*: he observes the starry sky and rejoices, because he sees in it the truth, what is behind it. Hearing them, "the halls of their father" rejoice as Homer's shepherd rejoices:

The halls of their father, loud-thundering Zeus, rejoice at the goddesses' clear voice spread abroad, and the peak of snowy Olympus rings, and the mansions of the gods. Making divine utterance, they celebrate first in their song the august family of gods, from the beginning, those whom Earth and broad Heaven begot, and the gods that were born from them, givers of blessings. Second they sing of Zeus, father of gods and men.

Hesiod, like the Bible, sings to glorify "things of the future and things that were aforetime," celebrates those who uniquely are eternal, the "blessed ones," and sings them "first and last always." And before them he sings, for a good hundred lines, the Muses, daughters of Zeus and Memory: Clio, Euterpe, Thaleia, Melpomene, Terpsichore, Erato, Polyhymnia, Ourania, and Calliope, "who is chief among them all." And "lovely is the sound they produce from their mouths," which tells "things of the future and things that were aforetime." Finally Hesiod can invoke them himself:

Farewell now, children of Zeus, and grant me delightful singing. Celebrate the holy family of immortals who are for ever, those who were born of Earth and Heaven and of black Night, and those whom the briny Sea fostered; and tell how the gods and the earth were born in the first place, and the rivers, and the boundless sea with its furious swell, and the shining stars and broad firmament above; and how they shared out their estate, and how they divided their privileges, and how they gained all the glens of Olympus in the first place. Tell me this from the beginning, Muses who dwell in Olympus, and say, what thing among them came first.

As moderns we might say that Hesiod's poem is essentially about poetry: a poem about the Muses (and Apollo, who, with them, is the progenitor of singers and lyre players), but also a magnificent cosmogony in mythic, sacred terms. It's not, of course, the story of a single God, the creator of all things, but of "things," of the gods who "were born" in the cosmos and "bore" others. Thus the cosmogony becomes a theogony:

First came the Chasm; and then broad-breasted Earth, secure seat for ever of all the immortals who occupy the peak of snowy Olympus; the misty Tartara in a remote recess of the broad-pathed earth; and Eros, the most handsome among the immortal gods, dissolver of flesh, who overcomes the reason and purpose in the breasts of all gods and all men.

Out of the Chasm came Erebos and dark Night, and from Night in turn came Bright Air and Day, whom she bore in shared intimacy with Erebos. Earth bore first of all one equal to herself, starry Heaven, so that he should cover her all about, to be a secure seat for ever for the blessed gods; and she bore the long mountains, pleasant haunts of the goddesses.

In the Beginning the Chasm "came into being" (the original verb is *genet'*, from the root *gígnomai,* "become"), and immediately afterward Earth, Tartara, and Eros. Both Aristotle and then Thomas Aquinas identify the last, Eros, the "most handsome among the immortal gods," as the most important entity of this opening: because, they say, Hesiod has understood that it's not sufficient to speak of merely material beginnings; there also has to be "some cause which moves and combines things." Eros, Love, is the beginning that truly inspires the cosmos.

The *Theogony* explains the beginnings of the world and its structure in terms of generation: the Chasm generates Erebos and Night, Earth generates starry Heaven, and so on. It also applies the concept of generation to personifications, like Strife and her descendants:

Hateful Strife bore painful Toil
Neglect, Starvation and tearful Pain,
Battles, Combats, Bloodshed and Slaughter,
Quarrels, Lies, Pretences and Arguments,
Disorder, Disaster—neighbors to each other—
And Oath.

The capacity to abstract, to create personifications, sig-
nifies a step forward in archaic thought, though it coexists
with the "multiple approach," which is absolutely typical
of Hesiod, allowing him, for example, to conceive of Night
both as the mother of Day and as what precedes day, both
as the daughter of the Chasm and as the product of the vis-
its of Uranus to Earth. Furthermore, the narrative structure
of the *Theogony* isn't based entirely on generation or on the
descent of some things from others. There are interrup-
tions and pauses in which particular problems are brought
into focus. A Hymn to Hecate is placed between the
descendants of Thea and Hyperion and those of Kronos
and Rhea, and narratives and descriptions of varying length
are inserted at crucial points: the story of Prometheus, the
Titanomachy, the section devoted to Tartarus, the
Typhonomachy.

The *Theogony*, in short, doesn't have a "classical," har-
monious architecture—of the type that characterizes the
Genealogie deorum gentilium of Boccaccio, dedicated, two
thousand years later, to the same theme—but has, rather, a
variable plot. It concludes with a couple of hundred lines
that almost all modern scholars consider spurious, and yet,
because they existed in the ancient world, and survived
into the modern, tenaciously attached to the body of the

work, must have a particular importance. The last generation of the *Theogony* leads in fact to the last of the semi-divine ancient heroes and to the West of Greek civilization: to Odysseus, the Etruscans, and the Phaeacians:

Circe, daughter of the Sun, the son of Hyperion, in shared intimacy with Odysseus the enduring of heart, bore Agrius and Latinus, the excellent and strong, who were lords of all the famous Tyrrhenians far away in a remote part of the Holy Isles. And Calypso, noble among goddesses, bore Nausithous and Nausinous to Odysseus in union of intimate desire.

It almost seems as if we were moving from the *Theogony* to proto-history: Nausithous is in fact the first king of the Phaeacians; Latinus—here, along with Agrius, taken as king of the Etruscans—is the eponymous hero of the Latins, neighbors of Rome, and Telegonus, the ignorant murderer of his father, Odysseus, will become the progenitor of the Claudians: that is, the Roman family that, with Tiberius, will inherit the empire from and with the *gens julia*, descendants of Augustus, Julius Caesar, and Aeneas.

Besides the *Theogony,* Hesiod is the author of, among other things, a poem entitled *The Works and Days*. If the *Theogony* covers the divine generations and concerns the beginning of the universe, *The Works and Days* is about the world of man and his destiny. After a very brief invocation to the Muses, Hesiod poses the central question of evil: his brother Perses, who shared his inheritance with him, has dissipated it, raising a "dispute" between them. The answer to the problem of evil is provided by three stories: the myth of

Prometheus and Pandora, the story of the five ages of man, and the "fable" of the sparrow and the nightingale. The first evil is the necessity for toil, Zeus's punishment for the gift of fire that Prometheus gives mankind. The others have been scattered through the world by the woman, Pandora, who is in part their cause, but they have also been influenced by the loss of happiness and the progressive decline and corruption of the human race over the five ages, and the failure to respect justice (the sparrow and the nightingale). Yet Hesiod also sees in the five ages a positive evolution, from a state of almost feral blessedness of the first race, beyond good and evil, to that, of the fifth, consisting in the capacity to be able to choose consciously one or the other.

The second part of *The Works and Days* provides advice and instructions for daily activities; practical lessons concerning work, that is, basically, how the cultivation of the fields should be organized during the various seasons of the year; and ethical maxims regarding the behavior and the well-being of every person. Here's an example of the latter:

Be a friend to him who is your friend,
And give your company to him that seeks it.
Give whoso gives, and give not whoso gives not:
to a giver one gives, to an ungiver none gives.

Perhaps the most beautiful instance of the former is the passage in which Hesiod shows his knowledge that the life of every day, of the seasons and the months, has to be governed by the phases of the night sky. For example, reaping should start when the Pleiades appear:

When the Pleiades born of Atlas rise before the sun, begin the reaping; the ploughing when they set.

For forty nights and days they are hidden, and again as the year goes round they make their first appearance at the time of iron-sharpening. This is the rule of the land, both for those who live near the sea and for those who live in the winding glens far from the swelling sea, a rich terrain.

The agricultural calendar begins and ends for Hesiod with the Pleiades ("When the Pleiades and the Hyades and mighty Orion are setting, then be thinking of ploughing in its season; and may the seed lodge firmly in the earth"), and going to sea should also be governed by the Pleiades:

If now the desire to go to sea (disagreeable as it is) has hold of you: when the Pleiades, running before Orion's grim strength, are plunging into the misty sea, then the blasts of every kind of wind rage; at this time do not keep ships on the wine-faced sea, but work the earth assiduously, as I tell you. Pull the ship on to land and pack it with stones all round to withstand the fury of the wet-blowing winds, taking out the plug so that heaven's rains do not cause rot.

The poem thus prescribes what to do in particular periods of the year, when certain constellations are visible in the sky. Eight hundred years later, Virgil's *Georgics* will also, at least in part, perform this task, which is to convey a technical and, at the same time, moral knowledge. In Hesiod's works, this type of knowledge seems to be placed on the same level as mythic knowledge, which investigates the origin of the universe in the divinities and the origins of evil in the story of Prometheus, in the ages of the world, and in the fable of the sparrow and the nightingale.

It's clear, in any case, that Hesiod is giving thoughtful attention to a whole series of issues that will later be central to philosophical meditation.

How did Greek culture move from its most ancient stage, in which thought is expressed in terms of myth (Homer and Hesiod), to the foundations of true philosophy, through the pre-Socratics and up to Socrates and Plato? Bruno Snell maintained that "it is impossible to radically separate rational enlightenment from religious illumination, teaching from conversion, or to understand the 'discovery of the spirit' as simply the invention and development of philosophical and scientific ideas. Rather, many of the fundamental contributions that the Greeks made to the development of European thought are introduced under forms that . . . we are used to associating with the religious sphere rather than with cultural history."[10]

The author Giorgio Colli, for his part, sought the origin of philosophy in the tradition of knowledge. Apollo and Dionysus stand at the beginning of knowledge: the oracle and the "mania," followed by the Mysteries of Eleusis, Orpheus, and Musaeus.[11]

Snell, in turn, published *Leben und Meinungen der Sieben Weisen,* or *The Lives and Opinions of the Seven Sages,* in which, using Diogenes Laërtius and other sources, he presented the "opinions" of Thales, Solon, Chilon, Pittacus, Bias, Cleobulus, and Periander (all of whom lived between the end of the seventh and the fifth century B.C.) as the link between knowledge and philosophy.

And in *The Masters of Truth in Archaic Greece*, Marcel

Detienne turns to, first, Nereus, the Old Man of the Sea of Homer and Hesiod, and Minos, the king of Crete, who unites in himself the functions of sovereignty, justice, and divination: both are bearers of an *alétheia* (truth) character-ized by wisdom.[12] To these I would add Tiresias, the prophet of the *Odyssey* and *Oedipus the King*, who "knows" things without having to get to that knowledge, unlike his adversary Oedipus, who must go through a labo-rious process of gaining knowledge, by uncovering evi-dence and making rational deductions.

Finally, to return to what the classics themselves have said about themselves, Aristotle has left us, in the first pages of the *Metaphysics*, an inestimably valuable recon-struction of the beginning of philosophy, and of Greek phi-losophy in particular. It's the story of a unique intellectual adventure, in which the search for *arkhé*, the beginning of things, becomes a thrilling and astute journey through the ideas and images that have formed our thought.

Everything begins with wonder, the true *arkhé* of the human gaze at the world. "Philosophizing" (*philosophéin*)—that is, love of knowledge—has its roots in wonder. Developing an idea already present in Plato's *Theaetetus*, Aristotle maintains that when human beings began to search for knowledge, "both now and originally," they wondered first about the *aporie*, or "puzzles," "that were to hand," and then moved on to more important questions, such as "about the affections of the moon, and events connected with the sun and the stars, and about the origins of the universe. And the man who is puzzled and amazed is thought to be igno-rant (hence the lover of stories is, in a way, a lover of wisdom, since a story is composed of wonders)."[13] It's clear that Aristotle is speaking here of remote times, when primitive humanity posed the first questions, but he also has in view the present, when the adolescent, the youth, or anyone undertaking research finds himself prey to wonder.

The mechanism that provokes love of knowledge is always the same, in the beginning and now and always: it's wonder at the things we don't know. In fact, it's important to note the extreme latitude of that wonder, which Aristotle extends to love for myth: "*Philosophus*," Thomas Aquinas comments fifteen centuries later, "*est aliqualiter philomythes, idest amator fabulae, quod proprium est poetarum.*" The philosopher is in some way a myth-lover, that is, a lover of the fabulous story, the myth, which belongs to the poets. Both the scientist (the "philosopher" is in the first place one who practices "natural philosophy," that is, investigates natural phenomena like the moon, the sun, the stars, and the very genesis of the cosmos), who will soon be the professional philosopher, and the artist find wonder to be the primary inspiration of their work.

After these general premises, Aristotle moves on to a historical review, and first discusses the philosophers who today are called "pre-Socratics." Aristotle maintains that most of them thought that the beginnings, or principles, of things were material, even if they had different opinions on the number and nature of such beginnings. Thales, "the introducer of this sort of philosophy," put water first, "perhaps drawing this supposition from seeing that the nourishment of all creatures is moist." Speaking of water, Aristotle declares that, according to some, "the very ancient thinkers and those long before the present generation and the first to reason about the gods" entertained the same opinion, making Ocean and Tethys the "parents of creation" (we saw it in the *Iliad*) and saying that "the oath of the gods was water": which they called Styx. Anaximenes and Diogenes, Aristotle continues, preferred air to water, Hippasus and Heraclitus fire, and Empedocles all the elements. Anaxagoras, finally, maintained that the number of principles was infinite.

Now the problems began. In most cases, generation and destruction arise from "some simple thing or from several," but why and what is the cause? Some of the thinkers who had hypothesized material causes began to wonder, and naturally couldn't conclude that it was the "substrate" that brings about change in itself: wood and bronze can't spontaneously change themselves, producing, respectively, a bed and a statue. Searching for the cause of these changes therefore means looking for "the beginning of the change." Hesiod himself, Aristotle states, must have realized this when, in the *Theogony,* he postulated Eros— loving desire—as *arché*, the beginning of entities. And Parmenides did the same. Thus Anaxagoras theorized the mind (*Nous*) as a device for the "making of the cosmos," and Empedocles Love and Strife, while the atomists Leucippus and Democritus, who assume as material causes the full (what is) and the empty (what is not), maintain that the differences are the causes of the other things.

Finally come the so-called Pythagoreans, who, having studied mathematics, "thought that the principles of mathematical entities were the principles of all entities," and since numbers are primary, "among these they seemed to observe many similarities with entities and things coming into being, rather than in fire and earth and water, so that such and such an affection of numbers is justice and such and such soul and mind and another time." Furthermore, seeing in numbers "the affections of harmonies," they decided that, since all other things were modeled on numbers and numbers themselves were primary in nature, "the elements of the numbers were the elements of things as a whole, and that the whole heaven was a harmony and a number."

Aristotle now has three remaining challenges: the Eleatics, Socrates, and Plato. It seems to me that he fails the first when he judges Xenophanes and Melissus "a little unsophisticated" and is struck but confused by Parmenides, whose position on the "one and nothing else" he appreciates but whom he likes less when, forced to follow the evidence, Parmenides considers that more things exist according to the senses and hence postulates two causes and two principles. Socrates, on the other hand, is avoided because he doesn't think about the whole of nature, though he is admired for his concern with ethical problems, in which he seeks universals, and for being the first to see the importance of "definitions." This opens the confrontation with his teacher, Plato. Aristotle believes that as a young man Plato encountered Cratylus and his Heraclitean positions, according to which "all perceptible things were in a permanent state of flux and . . . there was no knowledge of them." Plato thus shifted reality to the immutable world of Forms and imagined a divinity who shapes things, taking as a model the Forms themselves: which seems to be more poetic *mýthos* than scientific *lógos*. Maybe the grandiosity of the myth narrated in the *Timaeus* didn't escape Aristotle—it's one of the most fascinating ever invented—but in the *Metaphysics* he pressed Plato to propose his own vision of the science that understands principles and first causes, the "divine science" of metaphysics. "*Amicus Plato*," he would have said, "*sed magis amica veritas*": Plato is my friend, but dearer to me is truth.

In the *Poetics* Aristotle says that one could try to turn the *Histories* of Herodotus into verse, but they will never become poetry. The pre-Socratic thinkers composed in verse, in the hexameters of Homer and Hesiod. Rarely are their verses successful as song. But they demonstrate fully the spirit that moves them to investigate, the wonder that inspires love of knowledge. Naturally, it's impossible to enter into the details of their writings with the proper breadth here, but a couple of examples will be sufficient to show what sort of poetry they compose.

First, Parmenides, whose opening poem fragment reads:

The mares that carry me as far as ardor might go
Were bringing me onward, after having led me and set me down on
    the divinity's many-worded
Road, which carries through all the towns the man who knows.
It was on this road that I was being carried: for on it the much-knowing
    horses were carrying me,
Straining at the chariot, and maidens were leading the way.[14]

Riding in a chariot drawn by mares, Parmenides arrives in the presence of Dike, Justice, who possesses the keys to

truth and is able to teach the philosopher how to distin-
guish between true discourse and false. Guided by the
goddess, Parmenides embarks on the path of truth and
proclaims that only being exists, while non-being doesn't.
The frame of the poem is therefore allegorical, and
Parmenides' attempt to imitate Homer and Hesiod is real-
ized only in flashes, as in the fragment in which the goddess
promises the disciple that he will be instructed in all the
mechanisms of the cosmos:

You will know the aethereal nature, and in the aether all
The signs, and of the pure torch of the brilliant sun
The blinding works, and from where they are born,
And you will learn the recurrent works of the round-eyed moon
And its nature, and you will also know from where the sky, which is
    on both sides,
Was born and how Necessity led and enchained it
To maintain the limits of the heavenly bodies.

How the earth, the sun and the moon,
The aether in common and the heavenly milk, farthest
Olympus and the hot strength of the stars strove
To be born.

When he wants to, Parmenides can compose cosmic
poetry and in a few lines evoke the constellations, the sun, the
moon, the Milky Way, their Beginning and Necessity, which
guides them. So, too, Empedocles, who starts his *Poem* by
invoking the immortal Muse, asking her to preside when he
talks about the "happy gods," about the "elements not gen-
erated," about rancor and harmony. But Empedocles' imagi-
nation truly lights up, like Homer's (Aristotle in fact

described it as "Homeric"), in the passages where he can devote himself to epic-style similes, as when he deals with love, which acts on the elements, mixing and harmonizing them the way a painter mixes colors, or with the composition of the eyes, which is the work of "divine Aphrodite":

Just as when, thinking of setting forth, someone arms a lamp,
A gleam of bright fire across the stormy night,
Lighting a lamp-case to protect it against all kinds of winds,
Which scatters the breath of the blowing winds
While the light, leaping outward as far as possible,
Shines beyond the threshold with its unyielding rays—
In the same way, the ancient fire, confined in membranes and deli-
    cate linens,
Lay in wait for the round-eyed maiden [i.e. the opened pupil]:
These protected it against the depth of water flowing around,
While the fire gushed through outward as far as possible.
. . . the vision of "both" [eyes] becomes one.[15]

The surviving fragments of Heraclitus are not in verse and refer not to a poem but, rather, to a book, which he himself supposedly deposited in the temple of Artemis, in Ephesus, where he lived. Yet the fame of his sadness and melancholy (he is the "weeping philosopher"), his obscurity, ambiguity, and, at the same time, the force of penetration of his fragments have been such in the course of Western thought—from Plato to Plotinus, from Eckhart to Hegel, from Nietzsche to Heidegger—that his figure and his writings have assumed features of myth. If we consider that two fragments of Heraclitus were placed by Eliot facing the title page of *Four Quartets*—perhaps the most elevated poetic composition of the twentieth century—we will have an idea

of the presence and the importance of Heraclitus in litera-
ture. There is probably no greater icon of pre-Socratic
thought, apart from Empedocles, who, according to legend,
threw himself into Etna to prove that he was immortal or
vanished in a grand nocturnal eruption.

It's worth our while to look at some of these celebrated
fragments.[16] I would emphasize first of all those which have
to do with the soul and the self: "Traveling on every path,
you will not find the boundaries of soul by going; so deep
is its measure"; but also, obeying the precept of Delphi and
the order of Thales ("Know thyself"), "I searched myself";
and "To all men it is given to know themselves and not to
go beyond the limit." Then the eternal cycle of the *psyché*:
"For souls it is death to become water, and for water
death to become earth. Water comes into existence out of
earth, and soul out of water." Two remarkable observations
on our way of being: "Demon to each is his way of being";
"It is hard to fight with one's heart's desire, for it will
pay with soul for what it craves."

Immediately afterward I would place the fragments that
touch on the cosmos: "War is the father of all and the king
of all; some he has marked out to be gods and some to be
men, some he has made slaves and some free"; "Nature
loves to hide"; "This world, which is the same for all, was
made neither by a god nor by man, but it ever was, and is,
and shall be, ever-living Fire, in measures being kindled
and in measures going out"; "The limits of the East and
West are the Bear, and opposite the Bear is the boundary of
bright Zeus."

The paradoxes, integral or apparent: "Into the same

rivers we step and do not step; we are and we are not"; "Immortal mortals, mortal immortals, one living the others' death and dying the others' life"; "The road up and the road down is one and the same"; "The name of the bow is *bíos* and *biós* is life: but its work is death"; "The Lord whose is the oracle in Delphi neither declares nor hides, but sets forth by signs."

Some examples of literary and philosophical criticism, as Heraclitus practiced it, are opportune, since we're dealing with literature and philosophy: "Much learning does not teach understanding; else would it have taught Hesiod and Pythagoras, or, again, Xenophanes and Hecataeus"; "Homer deserved to be expelled from the lists and beaten, and Archilochus likewise"; "The teacher of most men is Hesiod. They think that he knew very many things, though he did not understand day and night. For they are one."

Even from these few citations we can understand the enormous appeal of Heraclitus, and the great passion he has for truth and philosophical inquiry. "Wisdom is one thing," he said. "It is to know the thought by which all things are steered through all things." But the best documents with which to conclude this brief excursus into the origins of thought in Greece have to do with Anaxagoras, the first philosopher who, coming from Ionia, lived in Athens, and in the age of Pericles. The first is a passage from *Eudemian Ethics*, in which Aristotle celebrates his cosmic passion; the second a sentence from Euripides, who, Diogenes Laërtius claims, was a student of Anaxagoras:

And so they tell us that Anaxagoras answered a man who was raising problems of this sort and asking why one should choose rather to be born than not: "for the sake of viewing the heavens and the whole order of the universe."[17]

Happy the man who has gained knowledge through inquiry, not aiming to trouble his fellow citizens, nor to act unjustly, but observing eternal nature's ageless order, the way it was formed, and whence and how. Such men are never inclined to practice shameful deeds.[18]

The pre-Socratic thinkers, as I've said, are only occasionally poets. The great poet of thought and philosophy is the Roman Lucretius, who lives his fairly short life in the first century B.C., four centuries after Heraclitus, Empedocles, and Parmenides (and three after Democritus), and who composes a formidable book of poetry that would have made any pre-Socratic envious, *De rerum natura*. To demonstrate what Lucretius does I will first use an oblique method, going through the book by way of images, then a direct method, concentrating on a couple of specific passages.

The invocation to Venus in *De rerum natura* is famous for its extraordinarily inspired celebration of life (whereas at the end of the work, in Book VI, there is a view of death):

O mother of the Roman race, delight
Of men and gods, Venus most bountiful,
You who beneath the gliding signs of heaven
Fill with yourself the sea bedecked with ships
And earth great crop-bearer, since by your power
Creatures of every kind are brought to birth
And rising up behold the light of sun;

From you, sweet goddess, you, and at your coming
The winds and clouds of heaven flee all away;
For you the earth well skilled puts forth sweet flowers;
For you the seas' horizons smile, and sky,
All peaceful now, shines clear with light outpoured.[19]

What interests me here is the images of the sea's smile and
the light that shines in the sky. The first derives from the
Prometheus of Aeschylus, in which the Titan chained to the
rock contemplates the ocean, which he calls "the countless
laughter of the sea's waves."[20] The image is so unusual, in
terms of tradition and of this particular tragedy, that the lis-
tener is momentarily stunned, and forgets everything he
knows about the sea as a physical entity, made of water and
mineral salts, and the sea as cradle of life, as vehicle of history,
navigation, transport, commerce, and instead luxuriates, for
a moment, in the surprising enigma of the poem. We ask our-
selves how waves can laugh or smile; and then agree that, cer-
tainly, if on a brilliantly sunny day we compare the sparkling
reflection of the swelling crests and foam to human senti-
ments, they can in fact look like a smile. The reader, now won
over by that image, will be reassured by Lucretius, who writes
that the waves of the sea "smile" at the generative power of
Venus: "*rident aequora ponti.*"

The crucial point here is the leap from the natural to the
human that the poem incites us to make. That leap, the
poetic metaphor, is the transfer of the qualities of one thing
to another; and wonder, as the purpose of the poem, finds
its starting point in the capacity to surprise. Well, Lucretius is
the master of this type of transfer. Here are two more exam-
ples. After the lines about the waves' smile, he continues to

celebrate Venus, who instills love in all creatures and through desire makes possible the perpetuation of the species. Now, using an expression borrowed from the *Annals* of the archaic poet Ennius, he writes, "Since you and only you are nature's guide, And nothing to the glorious shores of light [*dias in luminis oras*], Rises without you, nor grows sweet and lovely."

Lucretius is never banal, nor does he ever simply fall back on rhetorical expedients. Rather than use the cliché "coming into the light" for "being born," he intensifies Ennius' already potent expression, *in luminis oras* (to the shores of light), adding the qualifying adjective *dias*, divine, or glorious. Since Lucretius never makes a casual reference to the divine, we have to deduce that the adjective has a metaphoric function here, indicating not Olympus, the kingdom of the gods, but, rather, our earthly world. "Divine," or "glorious," must therefore stand for "sublime": so extraordinary and immense that it appears supernatural. The universe becomes a limitless background of light: in effect, expressed in the plural to emphasize its infiniteness, the divine runs aground on a shoal of light. The three words make the reader see light as a bright ocean that breaks on its own beach. Lucretius is so fond of the image that he repeats it nine times in the poem, and, along with his predecessor Ennius, he hands it down to Virgil, who (omitting *dias*) uses it in both the *Georgics* and the *Aeneid*.

Another example. In the line that immediately follows the one about the smile of the waves, the poet writes: "And sky, all peaceful now, shines clear with light outpoured (*placatumque nitet diffuso lumine caelum*)." But when, in

Book III of *De rerum natura*, Lucretius celebrates Epicurus, he returns to the splendor of the sky, translating a passage from Book VI of the *Odyssey*, in which Athena, after appearing in a dream to Nausicaa and inspiring in her the desire to take care of her trousseau, goes back up to Olympus. Homer says:

So the gray-eyed Athene spoke and went away from her
to Olympos, where the abode of the gods stands firm and unmoving
forever, they say, and is not shaken with winds nor spattered
with rains, nor does snow pile ever there, but the shining bright air
stretches cloudless away, and the white light glances upon it.

Lucretius rewrites it in an astonishing way, resorting to the smile of the sky:

The gods appear now and their quiet abodes
Which no winds ever shake, nor any rain
Falls on them from dark clouds, nor ever snow
Congealed with bitter frost with its white fall
Mars them; but always ever-cloudless air
Enfolds and smiles on them with bounteous light.

Et large diffuso lumine ridet, "and smiles on them with bounteous light": it's a stroke of genius that crosses over Homer by way of Aeschylus, making the sky equal in light to the sea, and the revelation of Epicurus equal to the fertility of Venus. The light we see now resembles Turner's. But the smile of the sea and the sky is no longer only a metaphor: it becomes the expression of the lovingness and kindness of nature.

With the next and last passage, from Book V of *De rerum natura*, we return to the Principle we started from in this chapter. Here we have scientific poetry intended to reduce to "true reason" what "the old Greek poets" had sung as myth. The *primordia rerum* (primal atoms), Lucretius writes, are not arranged each in its place "by design or intelligence," nor did they establish what movements should be made: rather, for a long time they clashed, repelled, joined, and scattered, "exploring every union and motion," until some met and joined suddenly (*repente*), often (*saepe*) becoming "the beginnings (*exordia*) of great things—of earth and sea and sky and living creatures":

Then not the sun's great wheel with bounteous light
Soaring aloft was seen, nor stars of heaven,
Nor sea nor sky nor earth at all nor air
Nor aught like things that in our world we know,
But a strange storm and surging mighty mass
Of atoms of all kinds in conflict locked
Created turmoil, in their intervals
Connections, courses, weights, blows, meetings, motions,
Because by reason of their different shapes and patterns
They could not all when joined together remain so,
Nor make the movements needed for their union.
Then parts began to separate, like things
Joining with like, and parcel out the world,
Fashion its limbs, set out its mighty parts—
That is, to set apart high heaven from earth,
And the sea apart, spreading its separate waters,
And apart too the pure and separate fires of ether.

The idea that rules this universe is based on diversity,

discord, chance, and the irregular movement of atoms, and has the great advantage (for moderns) of reflecting the conflict and disorder of the world. Virgil, adhering to an ideological-political order, the Augustan, much more rigid than the cosmos of Lucretius, re-echoes his lines in the famous song that he has Silenus utter in Eclogue VI, deriving causes from Empedocles as well as from Epicurus, from the Orphics as well as from Musaeus. And Ovid picks up some phrases from Lucretius in his version of origins, in the opening of the *Metamorphoses*. No one else, however, has invented a chaos that resembles a *nova tempestas*, a storm that is at the same time new and strange (coming after that of the atoms), and imminent, no one else a *moles coorta*: a mass, a "surging mighty mass" that bursts forth like a storm. There's no doubt: Lucretius is a poet who sings the origin of the cosmos even better than his Greek predecessors.

IV
THE BIRTH OF HISTORY

Herodotus of Halicarnassus here displays his inquiry, so that human achievements may not become forgotten in time, and great and marvelous deeds—some displayed by Greeks, some by barbarians—may not be without their glory; and especially to show why the two peoples fought with each other.[21]

These are the opening lines of the so-called *Histories* of Herodotus, "published" around—or a little before—425 B.C. I think we can say that it marks the birth of historiography, even though it was preceded by a slow development combining Orphism, the lyric poetry of Mimnermus and Callinus, the criticism of Epimenides, the *Genealogies* of Acusilaos and Hecateus, the *Periegesis* of the latter, and even Aeschylus' *The Persians*. This is a work of "research" (the literal meaning of the word *historia*), carried out by the author for the purpose of perpetuating the glory of "great and marvelous deeds" performed—it has to be emphasized—not only by the Greeks but also by the "barbarians," and in particular of remembering the causes of the wars between Greeks and barbarians.

Organized by Alexandrian grammarians into nine books—each dedicated to one of the Muses—the *Histories* covers a period of around eighty years, from the ascent of

Cyrus to the throne, in 560, to the final battle of the Persian-Greek conflict, in Mycale, in 479. But in reality the work includes much more, because to the central chronological thread Herodotus adds the history of the barbarians and the celebrated digressions, which range from the habits and customs of the Egyptians and the Scythians to discussions of geography, mythology, and religion, to cite only a few examples. The nine books begin with a prologue that examines the legendary causes of the wars between Greeks and Persians (abductions) and move on (I–IV) to describe events in the Persian Empire from the victory of Cyrus over the Lydian Croesus and the conquest of Assyria up to the failure to subdue the Massagetae (I); the history and customs of the Egyptians from the first king, Min, to the pharaoh Amasis, in the sixth century (II); the conquest of Egypt by Cambyses, the son of Cyrus (III); the rule of Darius, with the attempt to subdue the Scythians (IV); the first war between the Greeks and the Persians, with the revolt of Ionia and digressions on the history of Athens and Sparta (V); the rally of the Greeks, with the victory at Marathon (VI); the second Persian war, with the battles of Thermopylae, Salamis, Platea, and Mycale (VII–IX).

It's a grandiose and thrilling design, which Herodotus completes with judgment and restraint, while allowing himself all the observations and digressions that seem to him necessary ("From the beginning the story has required additions," he declares in Book IV), and combining the temporal dimension with the spatial, so that his history is a geography as well, often experienced in person or examined critically. "As to the writer who mentions the Ocean in this connection," he writes in Book II, "his account is a mere fairy tale depending upon an unknown quantity and cannot therefore be disproved by argument. I know myself of no river called Ocean, and can only suppose that Homer or some earlier poet invented the name and introduced it into poetry." In Book IV he argues with the traditional notion of the Hyperboreans (a people who lived "beyond the north wind," Boreas), claiming, ironically, that, by geometric parallel as advocated by the Ionian geographers, there should also exist a people called the "Hypernotians," who live beyond the south wind, Notus. He adds:

I cannot help laughing at the absurdity of all the map-makers—there are plenty of them—who show Ocean running like a river round a perfectly circular earth, with Asia and Europe of the same size. Let me spend a few words in giving a proper notion of the size and shape of these two continents.

Herodotus does precisely this, in fact, in the chapters immediately following, declaring openly that no one knows if Europe is bounded by waters on both the east and the north, and that we owe to the Persian Darius the exploration of the northern part of India. He goes so far as to correct popular geography *by means of history*, as when, also in Book IV, he describes the circumnavigation of Africa, entrusted to the Phoenicians by the Egyptian pharaoh Neco (the sovereign mentioned in Book II who wanted to dig the canal that would lead to the Red Sea). It's sensational news:

As for Libya we know that it is washed on all sides by the sea, except where it joins Asia, as was first demonstrated, so far as our knowledge goes, by the Egyptian king Neco, who, after calling off the construction of the canal between the Nile and the Arabian gulf, sent out a fleet manned by a Phoenician crew with orders to sail round and return to Egypt and the Mediterranean by way of the Pillars of Heracles. The Phoenicians sailed from the Red Sea into the southern ocean, and every autumn put in where they were on the Libyan coast, sowed a patch of ground and waited for next year's harvest. Then, having got their grain, they put to sea again, and after two full years rounded the Pillars of Heracles in the course of the third and returned to Egypt. These men made a statement which I do not myself believe, though others may, to the effect that as they sailed on a westerly course round the southern end of Libya, they had the sun on their right—to northward of them.

Herodotus exercises the same scrupulousness toward theogony and toward *arkhaiología*, that is, mythical stories of the origin of the divinities and the start of the wars between the Persians and the Greeks, and then he declares explicitly that, as for him, he "has to report what is said, but is not bound to believe it—and this statement holds for every story." As for Greek religion, he claims that it evolved in three phases: "undifferentiated and nameless gods; introduction of names and personalities from Egypt, thanks to the Pelasgians; systemization of this material by the Greeks, in particular Homer and Hesiod." In Book II of the *Histories* he writes:

But it was only—if I may so put it—the day before yesterday that the Greeks came to know the origin and form of the various gods, and whether or not all of them had always existed; for Homer and Hesiod are the poets who composed theogonies and described the gods for the Greeks, giving them all their appropriate titles, offices, and powers, and they lived, as I believe, not more than four hundred years ago. The poets who are said to have preceded them were, I think, in point of fact later. This is my personal opinion, but for the former part of my statement on these matters I have the authority of the priestesses of Dodona.

Herodotus presents the problem of how much trust to place in the ancient myths and poets, in particular Homer, in the first lines of the *Histories*, where he gives a concise account of the abductions of women for which each side blamed the other as the cause of hostilities between East and West. The Persians accuse the Phoenicians of abducting Io in Argos and carrying her off to Egypt, then they accuse the Greeks of kidnapping Europa in Tyre, in Phoenicia. The Greeks were then supposedly guilty of a second wrong, the abduction of Medea from Colchis, for which they refused to make reparations. A generation later, here's Alexander (Paris), the son of Priam, who "was inspired by these stories to steal a wife for himself out of Greece, being confident that he would not have to pay for the venture any more than the Greeks had done." Paris abducted Helen, and the Greeks asked for her back by diplomatic means. The Trojans then reproached them for kidnapping Medea; the result was war and, in the end, the destruction of the city. Thus the Persians consider the conquest of Troy the start of their enmity toward the Greeks (while the Phoenicians, for their part, maintain that Io wasn't raped but slept with the master of the ship in Argos and, getting pregnant, left with the Phoenicians in order not to be discovered).

Herodotus considers this legendary and almost novelistic plot of abductions irrelevant: "for my part," he writes at the start of Book I, "I have no intention of passing judgment on its truth or falsity. I prefer to rely on my own knowledge, and to point out who it was in actual fact that first injured the Greeks; then I will proceed with my history." The person in question is Croesus, the king of Lydia, and the *Histories* begins right afterward with his story. But Herodotus doesn't ever forget either the Trojan War or Homer. When Xerxes assembles a gigantic army to attack Greece, the historian notes, in Book VII, that not even the army that Agamemnon and Menelaus led to Troy was so large. As for Homer, in Book II, devoted to Egypt, Herodotus reckons with the legend that Helen never reached Troy but stayed in Egypt instead, where Paris had arrived in the course of his journey by sea from Sparta to Troy, and where Proteus obliged him to leave the woman he had obtained by offense and betrayal. This is the version of the story that the Egyptian priests, for whom Herodotus has the greatest respect, tell. Homer, the historian then says, knew this perfectly well, but since it was less "suitable for epic poetry than the one he actually used, he left indications that it was not unknown to him": as shown by certain passages of the *Iliad* and the *Odyssey* that Herodotus cites and which, in his view, prove unequivocally that the *Cypria*, a lost epic poem attributed to Stasinus, whose events would precede those narrated in the *Iliad,* is not by Homer but by someone else.

Passages like these are, on the one hand, a great exercise in comparative mythology (the abductions) set against the factual truth (the responsibility of Croesus), and, on the other, a bit of high literary criticism: the affair of Helen in

Egypt isn't suitable for epic poetry (Euripides uses it, but in a very different way, in *Helen*), which evidently needs a story that has as its center a complex narrative and, above all, as we saw in the first chapter, Helen's "supreme" beauty. A little later in Book II, Herodotus deconstructs the logic of the epic poem. He adheres to the version of the Egyptian priests, he says, because "had Helen really been in Troy, she would have been handed over to the Greeks with or without Paris' consent. For I cannot believe that either Priam or any other kinsman of his was mad enough to be willing to risk his own and his children's lives and the safety of the city, simply to let Paris continue to live with Helen." Even if "that had been their feeling when the troubles began," they would surely have given her back later. The Trojans died every day by the hundreds, every day ("if we may believe the epic poems") at least two or three or even more of Priam's own sons were killed: even if it had been Priam who lived with Helen, he would have given her back just to be released from the siege and the continuous slaughter. And then the heir to the throne wasn't Paris but Hector, and it wasn't right for Hector to give in to his brother, who was committing an injustice, especially "as it was the cause of much distress both to himself and to every other Trojan besides." But, Herodotus concludes, the fact is that the Trojans couldn't give Helen back because they didn't have her, and the Greeks couldn't believe them even if they were telling the truth: "I do not hesitate to declare that the refusal of the Greeks to believe it came of divine volition in order that their utter destruction might plainly prove to mankind that great offences meet with great punishments at the hands of God. This, then, is my own interpretation."

We can imagine the effect of such a speech on the Athenian public, for Herodotus in fact gave lectures taken from the material of his research. The *Iliad* was sacred, and questioning its arguments in favor of drivel spread by foreign priests would have been, precisely, a sacrilege. It's true that in the *Iliad* itself the old people of Troy, at first enchanted by Helen's beauty when she appears nearby on the walls, then say to each other that it would be better to give her back. And Hector, at the decisive moment of his fight with Achilles, thinks, in the grip of terror, that he could offer to return her. But in the *Iliad* Helen is there, in Troy, terribly like a goddess: giving her back is unmentionable. Herodotus challenges the Homeric fiction, starting from the "negationist" hypothesis that Helen had never reached Troy: he introduces the reality principle into the poetic myth, and in fact twice repeats that this is only his opinion, his point of view. For the theology that Priam gives voice to in the *Iliad*, welcoming Helen on the walls ("for me you have no blame, the gods have the blame / who stirred up the wretched war of the Achaeans"), he substitutes a retributive version in which the death of so many Trojans "came of divine volition" to make it clear to men that for great wrongs the punishment, too, is great.

For the reader of the *Histories*, these discussions have the same fascination as the descriptions of places and customs, along with many of the "stories" that they offer. The former stimulate our more sophisticated intellectual appetite, the others the same appetite and the same curiosity but on a sensory level. Who could resist the descriptions of Babylon and the so-called Tower of Babel in Book I and of the pyramid of Cheops in Book II: the former massive, "one furlong square," with another tower above it, and then a third, and yet another, up to eight, and at the top is a temple, and inside the temple a large couch, and next to it a golden table; the second constructed in steps by means of incredible contrivances that rise from step to step. But the customs of some Indian peoples, in Book III, exercise, in the realm of horror and the macabre, a very particular attraction:

Another tribe further to the east is nomadic, known as the Padaei; they live on raw meat. Among their customs, it is said that when a man falls sick, his closest companions kill him, because, as they put it, their meat would be spoilt if he were allowed to waste away with disease. The invalid, in these circumstances, protests that there is nothing the matter with him—but to no purpose. His friends refuse to accept his protestations, kill him and hold a banquet. Should the sufferer be a woman, her woman friends deal with her in the same way. If anyone is lucky enough to live to an advanced age, he is offered in sacrifice before the banquet—this, however, rarely happens, because most of them will have had some disease or other before they get old, and will consequently have been killed by their friends.

Reading Herodotus, we are amazed by the variety of his interests and the power of his curiosity. There is no detail that escapes him, that he doesn't want to investigate—he could by rights call himself not only "the father of history" but also "the father of micro history." And even the father of novelized history: when, for example, in Book I, he recounts the intricate plot of Astyages, Harpagos, and

Cyrus, he doesn't simply go from the dynasty of the Medes to that of the Persians but pauses for many chapters on an affair full of dreams and interpretations, of children exposed on a desert mountaintop and exchanged, of recognitions and revelations, of human flesh boiled, roasted, and eaten.

But his descriptions of the battles and catastrophes that mark the war between the Greeks and the Persians are also memorable: Marathon, the Thermopylaes, Salamis, Platea. The images of Leonidas' three hundred who, having lost their spears, fight with swords, with hands, with teeth before succumbing, one by one (what Longinus calls hyperbole), of the Acropolis burning in a deserted Athens, and, finally, of Xerxes, who, sitting on the throne on the summit of Mt. Hegaleus, contemplates the disaster of the Persian fleet at Salamis—these images are indelibly fixed in the minds of readers of the *Histories*.

There are phrases that we remember, too, because, underscoring the differences between Greeks and barbarians, they establish precise identities and the essential points of a credo that is not only political but regards an entire civilization. I'll choose some from Book VII, which is the most dense in this respect. Let's look at the Spartan Demaratos' answer to Xerxes, who has said he is sure that the Greeks, divided, will not fight against an infinitely more numerous army that, under the command of a single man, is stronger than they are. Demaratos answers:

Personally I do not claim to be able to fight ten men—or two; indeed I should prefer not even to fight with one. But should it be necessary—

should there be some great cause to urge me on—then nothing would give me more pleasure than to stand up to one of those men of yours who claim to be a match for three Greeks. So it is with the Spartans; fighting singly, they are as good as any, but fighting together they are the best soldiers in the world. They are free—yes—but not entirely free; for they have a master, and that master is Law, which they fear much more than your subjects fear you. Whatever this master commands, they do; and his command never varies: it is never to retreat in battle, however great the odds, but always to remain in formation, and to conquer or die.

Jacqueline de Romilly writes that this passage is the culmination of the "discovery of the law" that characterizes fifth-century Greece. For the Spartans, the *nómos*, the law, is, along with freedom, a more powerful sovereign than Xerxes. Later, the Spartans are entertained by Hydarnes, the Persian in command "of the whole Asiatic seaboard," who says that if they surrender they may govern the Greek provinces in the name of the king. They reply: "Hydarnes, the advice you give us does not spring from a full knowledge of the situation. You know one half of what is involved, but not the other half. You understand well enough what slavery is, but freedom you have never experienced, so you do not know if it tastes sweet or bitter. If you ever did come to experience it, you would advise us to fight for it not with spears only but with axes too."

Greek identity is defined in terms of freedom and law, as opposed to the invader, who knows only servitude and absolute rule. The wars against the Persians are, as these passages clearly demonstrate, conflicts of mentality: the Asians can't understand how a people can prefer freedom to honors and promotions from the king, and at the cost of bloody battles destined to defeat anyway; for them law is the command of that king.

For Herodotus, it's not enough to present the Spartans as defenders of Hellas. He is well aware—elaborating at length a series of tactical considerations—that without the simultaneous and decisive resistance of Athens the invaders would have conquered Greece. So he intervenes in the first person and develops a perfect logic. "At this point," he states, "I find myself compelled to express an opinion which I know most people will object to; nevertheless, as I believe it to be true, I will not suppress it." If the Athenians, he continues, had abandoned their land or had surrendered to Xerxes, no one would have challenged him on the sea. And on land the Spartans would have remained alone, to die nobly or make a pact with Xerxes. All Greece would then have ended up in the hands of the Persians:

In view of this, therefore, one is surely right in saying that Greece was saved by the Athenians. It was the Athenians who held the balance: whichever side they joined was sure to prevail. It was the Athenians, too, who, having chosen that Greece should live and preserve her freedom, roused to battle the other Greek states which had not yet submitted. It was the Athenians who—after the gods—drove back the Persian king.

History is made like this as well, with respect for the "true" (or, as the late David Asheri, a classicist who taught and wrote at the Hebrew University of Jerusalem, put it, the "more or less likely") and the development of reason: not only by means of direct knowledge (*ópsis*) and oral testimony (*akoé*) but also by means of rational reflection, and by having in mind both the "cyclical nature of human events" that (in the words of Croesus to Cyrus) "doesn't allow the same ones always to have good fortune," and wise "divine providence" that, as the author declares in Book III, rules universal history and biological equilibrium—"after the gods," of course, as Herodotus writes in the passage I've just cited.

Herodotus was still living, and his *Histories* had been circulating for some time, when the second great historian of classical Greece entered the scene, the Athenian Thucydides. The Persian Wars ended in 479, and barely fifty years later (in 431, when Herodotus was still alive) war erupted between Athens and Sparta, in the Peloponnese, and didn't end until 404. Thucydides narrates the outbreak and the events up to 411, while the last years are the subject of the first two books of Xenophon's *Hellenica*. Thucydides' purpose here is different, because he is concerned with a war that is taking place in the present, and entirely within Greece, and so his attitude is different, too, from that of Herodotus, whom he cites (and sometimes mocks).

There is no reference to myth or any divine intervention in the *Peloponnesian War*. The causes of events are purely human, and Thucydides tries to confront them as objectively as possible: "The war was begun," he writes, "by the Athenians and Peloponnesians when they broke the Thirty Years Treaty which they had established after the capture of Euboea."[22] The reasons for war, on both sides, were certainly numerous, but Thucydides understands immediately the "real reason, true but unacknowledged." It was "the growth of Athenian power and Spartan fear of it" which "forced the war." And this attitude became the fundamental model first for the Greek and Latin historians, and then for modern historians. One feels it in the tone in which Thucydides' exposition opens:

Thucydides of Athens wrote this history of the war fought against each other by the Peloponnesians and the Athenians. He began his work right at the outbreak, reckoning that this would be a major war and more momentous than any previous conflict. There were two grounds for this belief: both sides were at the full height of their power and their resource for war, and he saw the rest of the Greeks allying with one or the other, either immediately or in intent. This was in fact the greatest disturbance to affect the Greek and a good part of the non-Greek world, one might even say the majority of mankind.

Here it is, the war of the Peloponnese between Athens and Sparta: the central event not only of Greek history but of all mankind is the model that Thucydides wants to propose to us. Greece is the most civilized country of his era, a fact we can still agree on. What happens in Greece: the division between Athens and Sparta, which didn't exist until the Peloponnesian War, since the two had fought together against the Persian invasion; the separation, the split, the hostilities, the open conflict ending with the defeat of the apparently more civilized and more cultured Athens, which will have a greater consequence in the history both of Rome and of the entire West—this is Thucydides' grand theme.

Tackling this theme, the historian briefly summarizes

the earlier history of Greece, purposely avoiding the style of the poets, "who exaggerate" events, tell "glorified tales," and that of the prose writers, "whose stories are written more to please the ear than to serve the truth." No: he "will find" events "using the clearest evidence available," and he will rely on two methods of reconstruction: the facts, not obtained from whoever happens along but evaluated rigorously both when witnessed in the first person and when learned from others; and speeches uttered by both sides and written "to say broadly what I supposed would have been needed on any given occasion, while keeping as closely as I could to the overall intent of what was actually said." In the *War*, that is, the speeches tend to acquire the probabilistic status of facts, reflecting, in the author's view, the leading ideas, the fundamental thought, not only of the characters on the scene but of entire communities. Too bad if this method of proceeding makes him unpopular with the public:

It may be that the lack of a romantic element in my history will make it less of a pleasure to the ear: but I shall be content if it is judged useful by those who will want to have a clear understanding of what happened—and, such is the human condition, will happen again at some time in the same or a similar pattern. It was composed as a permanent legacy, not a showpiece for a single hearing.

Thucydides calls his work "a permanent legacy," because the facts and speeches set forth by him are based on laws founded on what is proper to man, to "human nature." And human nature possesses, above all, a desire for "growth," for reinforcement, for expansion, on the level of both the individual and the community. And it's this desire that, in the end, leads to conflict with the other, to war. The desire for honor and prestige, and usefulness, also leads to war, while fear leads to defense. And yet for both sides war is based on absolutely similar material grounds: arms and, behind them, financial availability, money. The Spartan Archidamus and the Athenian Pericles say it openly, in Book I, at the start of the huge conflict.

Pericles' speech to the Athenians later, in Book II, regarding the first men fallen in the war, goes far beyond the simple material horizon. In that famous speech Pericles praises the type of government that Athens has devoted itself to and the way of life of its inhabitants:

"I shall not mention our achievements in war, the campaigns which won us each addition to the empire, our own or our fathers' spirited resistance to the attacks of Greek or barbarian enemies—I have no wish to delay you with a long story which you know already. But before I pass on to the praise of the dead, I shall describe first the principles of public life which set us on our way, and the political institutions and national character which took us on to greatness. I think this a suitable subject for the present occasion, and it could be of benefit for this whole gathering, foreigners as well as citizens, to hear this account.

"We have a form of government which does not emulate the practice of our neighbours: we are more an example to others than an imitation of them. Our constitution is called a democracy because we govern in the interests of the majority, not just the few. Our laws give equal rights to all in private disputes, but public preferment depends on individual distinction and is determined largely by merit rather than rotation: and poverty is no barrier to office, if a man despite his humble condition has the ability to do some good to the city. We are open and free in the conduct of our public affairs and in the uncensorious way we observe the habits of each other's daily lives: we are not angry with our neighbour if he indulges his own pleasure, nor do we put on the disapproving look which falls short of punishment but can still hurt."

Democracy, freedom, equality, tolerance: we hear these proclaimed openly here for the first time. They are accompanied by the celebration of taste and the beautiful, education to intellectual and physical pleasures, the development of personality. Pericles delineates in a few words that unique measure of good, beautiful, and just that marks Athenian civilization.

And yet Pericles has barely finished speaking, in Thucydides' chronicle-history, when the Peloponnesians, under the command of Archidamos, invade Attica and ravage it, and during their occupation the plague breaks out in Athens, which sweeps away a good part of the Athenian population, including Pericles himself. This first plague in Western literature inspires Lucretius and returns in the pages of Boccaccio, Manzoni, and Camus. The description of the plague in Thucydides' *War* is one of the most famous passages of the work, in which we see simultaneously the force of the writing, the devastating power of the disease, and the explosion of *týche*—chance—that dominates human affairs:

The original outbreak, it is said, was in Ethiopia, the far side of Egypt: the plague then spread to Egypt and Libya, and over much of the King's territory. It fell on the city of Athens suddenly. The first affected were the inhabitants of the Peiraeus, who went so far as to allege that the Peloponnesians had poisoned the wells (at that time there were no fountains in the Peiraeus). Afterwards the plague reached the upper city too, and now the number of deaths greatly increased. Others, doctors or laymen, can give their individual opinions of the likely origin of the plague, and of the factors which they think significant enough to have had the capacity to cause such a profound change. But I shall simply tell it as it happened, and describe the features of the disease which will give anyone who studies them some prior knowledge to enable recognition should it ever strike again. I myself caught the plague, and witnessed others suffering from it. It so happened that this year was commonly agreed to have been particularly free from other forms of illness, though anyone with a previous condition invariably developed the plague. The other victims were in good health until, for no apparent cause, they were suddenly afflicted. The first symptoms were a high fever in the head and reddening and inflammation of the eyes; then internally the throat and tongue began to bleed and the breath had an unnaturally foul smell. There followed sneezing and hoarseness of voice, and shortly the affliction moved down to the chest accompanied by a violent cough. When it settled in the stomach the turmoil caused there led to the voiding of bile in every form for which the doctors have a name, all this with great pain.

Thucydides' chilling medical precision doesn't stop until he has described all the symptoms and developments: unbearable burning heat, impossibility of resting, insomnia, a headache that descends into the abdominal cavity and the extremities, the loss of genitals, hands and feet, eyes, of memory and the sense of self. "The pathology of the disease defied explanation," the historian writes. Discouragement and despair among those who were stricken, inevitable contagion among those who offer help, the chaos of bodies piled everywhere: and "increased lawlessness." The wealthy who die suddenly and the poor who take possession of their wealth, abandonment to "satisfactions that were quick and pleasurable," the failure of every constraint in the face of human or divine law.

After reading a passage like that we hardly expect that the author will present a real dialogue, as if it were a dramatic exchange from Sophocles' *Philoctetes* or *Antigone*. But Thucydides performs that tour de force as well, and the famous dialogue between the Athenian ambassadors and the Melian counselors, who discuss in detail the Athenians' attack on the neutrality of the island, exposes the arguments of imperialism, its lack of limits, the cruelty it entails in the name of the law of the stronger.

The Athenians proclaim, "We believe it of the gods, and we know it for sure of men, that under some permanent compulsion of nature wherever they can rule, they will. . . . We did not make this law," they say; "it was already laid down, and we are not the first to follow it; we inherited it as a fact, and we shall pass it on as a fact to remain true for ever; and we follow it in the knowledge that you and anyone else given the same power as us would do the same."

It's the inexorable law of power, which the Athenians themselves will experience at the end of the war, when they are decisively defeated first in Sicily, then on their own ground. Here they are, now, locked up in the prisons of Syracuse, at the end of Book VII. The Peloponnesian War lasted ten more years, but this is a description from the grave:

The prisoners in the quarries were harshly treated by the Syracusans in the early days of their captivity. Large numbers were confined in a deep and narrow space. Direct sun and suffocating heat, with no shelter, oppressed them first by day, and then the autumnal nights that followed brought cold and a contrasting extreme of temperature which ruined their health. In such a cramped space they had to do everything just where they were: and with the dead bodies piling up too (men dying of their wounds, through the changes of temperature, and other such causes), the stench was unbearable. They were also afflicted by hunger and thirst . . . for some seventy days: thereafter the Syracusans sold the others as slaves, but kept in that confinement the Athenians and any Sicilian or Italian Greeks who had fought on their side. The total number of state prisoners taken is hard to establish exactly, but was not less than seven thousand.

This proved the most significant occurrence in the whole of this war, and, it seems to me, in the whole of recorded Greek history—unparalleled triumph for the victors, and unparalleled disaster for the vanquished. This was, as they say, "total annihilation." Beaten in every way on every front, extreme miseries suffered on an extreme scale, and army, fleet, and everything else destroyed, few out of all those many made their return home.

Such were the events in Sicily.

V
TRAGEDY AND JUSTICE

Ten years since the great contestants
of Priam's right,
Menelaus and Agamemnon, my lord,
Twin-throned, twin-sceptered, in twofold power
of kings from God, the Atreidae,
put forth from this shore
the thousand ships of the Argives,
the strength and the armies.
Their cry of war went shrill from the heart,
as eagles stricken in agony
for young perished, high from the nest
eddy and circle
to bend and sweep of the wings' stroke,
lost far below
the fledglings, the nest, and the tendance.
Yet someone hears in the air, a god,
Apollo, Pan, or Zeus, the high
thin wail of these sky-guests, and drives
late to its mark
the Fury upon the transgressors.
So drives Zeus the great guest god
the Atreidae against Alexander:
for one woman's promiscuous sake
the struggling masses, legs tired,
knees grinding in dust,
spears broken in the onset.

Danaans and Trojans
they have it alike. It goes as it goes
now. The end will be destiny.
You cannot burn flesh or pour unguents,
not innocent cool tears,
that will soften the gods' stiff anger.[23]

This is what the Chorus sings right after the start of the *Oresteia* (apparently the last tragic trilogy of Aeschylus), which was presented, along with the satiric drama *Proteus*, at the Festival of Dionysus in Athens in 458 B.C., and which won first prize. I like to think that these words mark the birth of tragedy in Greece: naturally, and significantly, with a return to the Trojan War and the curse that it constitutes for the House of Atreus, for Menelaus and Agamemnon. The *Oresteia* is the story of Orestes, but it is linked to the story of his father, Agamemnon, and to the Erinyes' persecution of Orestes himself in the last drama of the trilogy, *The Eumenides*.

"It goes as it goes now," the Chorus says. "The end will be destiny": things are as they are, but will happen as fate has established. Everything is bound by necessity and by fate: *móira*. Agamemnon, bringing with him as a slave Cassandra, the prophetess daughter of Priam, returns to Argos after the victory in Troy and is immediately killed in the bath by his wife, Clytemnestra, and her lover, Aegisthus. According to the law of retaliation, his son Orestes, who is absent from Argos, must therefore carry out *némesis*, revenge: punish the killers of his father. In the second play of the trilogy, *The Libation Bearers*, Orestes returns to Argos, is recognized by his sister Electra, and the two, joining forces, kill their mother and

Aegisthus. But killing the mother requires, in turn, revenge. It's an endless chain, into which the Furies, the Erinyes, are sent by a god—Zeus, Apollo, or Pan—to punish *each* of the transgressors, from Atreus to Agamemnon, from Clytemnestra to Orestes. At the end of the trilogy, the Erinyes pursue Orestes, who will at last find refuge in Athens. The chain of crime, anger, and revenge that dominates the *Oresteia*, over which *móira* and *némesis* wield their oppressive power, is truly tremendous. We need only listen to the few characters on the stage, especially the women: Clytemnestra, Cassandra, Electra. They clearly dominate the male characters; they "perform" the action. Cassandra, the virgin prophetess daughter of Priam, carried as a slave to Greece, "hears" and "sees" what is happening in the palace of Argos:

CASSANDRA:
Ah, for shame, what can she purpose now?
What is this new and huge
stroke of atrocity she plans within the house
to beat down the beloved beyond hope of healing?
Rescue is far away.

CHORUS:
I can make nothing of these prophecies. The rest
I understood; the city is full of the sound of them.

CASSANDRA:
So cruel then, that you can do this thing?
The husband of your own bed
to bathe bright with water—how shall I speak the end?
This thing shall be done with speed. The hand gropes now, and the other
hand follows in turn.

CHORUS:
> No, I am lost. After the darkness of her speech
> I go bewildered in a mist of prophecies.

CASSANDRA:
> No, no, see there! What is that thing that shows?
> Is it some net of death?
> Or is the trap the woman there, the murderess?
> Let now the slakeless fury in the race
> Rear up to howl aloud over this monstrous death.

Cassandra's gift of prophecy is, as it was in Troy, a terrible misfortune, and compels us to see the crime through her mind and voice—as, to an even greater degree, we also do in Seneca's *Agamemnon*. This is infinitely more effective than presenting it directly on the stage: where, soon afterward, we'll hear only the voice of Agamemnon, which resounds like an echo of the prophecy.

Clytemnestra, on the other hand, claims that she is justified in killing her husband. Ten years of unfaithfulness with Aegisthus are not enough: the excuse she offers is punishment for Agamemnon's sacrifice of their daughter Iphigenia, which, the seers said, was necessary so that the Greek fleet could depart for Troy:

No shame, I think, in the death given
this man. And did he not
first of all in this house wreak death
by treachery?
The flower of this man's love and mine,
Iphigenia of the tears
he dealt with even as he has suffered.
Let his speech in death's house be not loud.

With the sword he struck,
with the sword he paid for his own act.

"He paid for his own act." It is, precisely, the law of retaliation: eye for an eye, tooth for a tooth: as at the beginning of the Hebrew Scripture, in the Bible. The Chorus, which represents the people of Argos, and in particular the old people, is horrified by the crime, but in fact shares the logic of the law. When Clytemnestra, condemned to exile by Argos for the murder, refuses to accept it, the Chorus returns to that same law:

Great your design, your speech is a clamor of pride.
Swung to the red act drives the fury within your brain
signed clear in the splash of blood over your eyes.
Yet to come is stroke given for stroke
vengeless, forlorn of friends.

It's not clear if the Chorus is alluding to punishment by exile, which Clytemnestra has just been threatened with, or to the revenge of Orestes, but the point is that even in the first case punishment for the murder is translated into an exchange, a repayment of the crime, *stroke for stroke*. Aegisthus is equal to his lover. He attributes the part that he had in the murder of Agamemnon to the same law. In killing Agamemnon, in fact, Aegisthus revenges the crimes that Atreus, the father of Agamemnon, committed against his father, Thyestes, and in particular the horrendous banquet at which Atreus had prepared for Thyestes the flesh of his own children, and which we will witness, with revulsion, in Seneca's *Thyestes*:

"Hail gracious light of the day of retribution! At last the hour has come when I can say that the gods who avenge mortal men look down from on high upon the crimes of earth. Now that, to my joy, I behold this man lying here in a robe spun by the Avenging Spirits and making full payment for the deeds contrived in craft by his father's hand." . . .

"For Atreus, lord of this land, this man's father, challenged in his sovereignty, drove forth, from city and from home, Thyestes, who (to speak it clearly) was my father and his own brother. And when he had come back as a suppliant to his hearth, unhappy Thyestes secured such safety for his lot as not himself to suffer death and stain with his blood his native soil. But Atreus, the godless father of this slain man, with welcome more hearty than kind, on the pretence that he was cheerfully celebrating a happy day by serving meat, served up to my father as entertainment a banquet of his own children's flesh. The toes and fingers he broke off . . . sitting apart. And when all unwittingly my father had quickly taken servings that he did not recognize, he ate a meal which, as you see, has proved fatal to his race. Now, discovering his unhallowed deed, he uttered a great cry, reeled back, vomiting forth the slaughtered flesh, and invoked an unbearable curse upon the line of Pelops, kicking the banquet table to aid his curse, 'thus perish all the race of Pleisthenes!' This is the reason that you see this man fallen here. I am he who planned this murder and with justice. For together with my hapless father he drove me out, me his third child, as yet a baby in swaddling-clothes. But grown to manhood, justice has brought me back again. Exile though I was, I laid my hand upon my enemy, compassing every device of cunning to his ruin. So even death would be sweet to me now that I behold him in justice's net."[24]

Aegisthus, like Clytemnestra before him, invokes Dike herself, Justice in person. It's evident that the two agree about its meaning, and that it leads to the hoped-for result: for them "doing justice" means getting rid of the one who was guilty of a crime, directly or indirectly, in person or through heredity—Iphigenia, Atreus.

Justice then coincides with nemesis, revenge, and, in the final analysis, with the force used in the act of revenge. Because, obviously, Orestes and Electra, too, will be able to invoke Dike and claim that the punishment of Clytemnestra and Aegisthus is just. "Warstrength shall collide with warstrength; right with right." The Chorus also says it in *The Libation Bearers*, the second play of the trilogy, when Orestes returns to Argos to perform his duty as avenger:

Almighty Destinies, by the will
of Zeus let these things
be done in the turning of Justice.
For the word of hatred spoken, let hate
be a word fulfilled. The spirit of Right
cries out aloud and extracts atonement
due: blood stroke for the stroke of blood
shall be paid. Who acts, shall endure. So speaks
the voice of the age-old wisdom.

The Furies, in turn, will be able to pursue Orestes for the matricide, crying revenge and, through that, justice toward her. The chain will end only when that particular lineage is gone or when one of its links is revealed to be inexorably, definitively stronger than another: preceding, successive, or contemporary.

The system essentially hurtles into the inextricable conflicts of tragedy: from time immemorial, or three generations, as the Chorus maintains. It seems to possess the inexorability of life, and is many times called "sorrow," "suffering," "pain," like life. Certainly, the debate between Electra, Orestes, and the Chorus about Justice stands at the center of *The Libation Bearers*, where it culminates in two fundamental points. The first is at the beginning, when Electra says, "There has been wrong done. I ask for right. Hear me, Earth. Hear me, grandeurs of Darkness!" and the Chorus responds with an image of unusual violence:

It is but law that when the red drops have been spilled
upon the ground they cry aloud for fresh
blood. For the death act calls out on Fury
to bring out of those who were slain before
new ruin on ruin accomplished.

Áte upon *áte*, misfortune upon misfortune, ruin upon ruin: that's the law, the *nómos* of human existence. Orestes grasps the idea completely soon afterward, when he sees the irremediable conflict between justice and justice, and he predicts that "warstrength shall collide with warstrength." Electra, in turn, prays that the gods will "be just." But the Chorus replies by returning attention to the "pain" of the family lineage, "O pain grown into the race and blood-dripping stroke," and commenting desperately: "grinding cry of disaster, moaning and impossible weight to bear. Sickness that fights all remedy."

Justice brings grief, suffering, ruin. Paradoxically, there is a moment in the *Oresteia*, before the resolution imposed by Athena at the end, that suggests a glimmer of hope. It's a moment of knowledge and reunion, when, many years after the murder of Agamemnon, Orestes returns to his homeland. First, he has to be recognized by his sister Electra, whom he needs in order to carry out his revenge. Aeschylus then constructs a formidable scene of recognition, which has echoed down the millennia from the fifth century B.C. to our own twenty-first century.

When Electra arrives to pour libations on her father's tomb, she finds a lock of hair on the grave and, on the ground, some footprints. Apprehensively, she observes that no one would have cut it except her: "Those others, whom it would have become, are full of hate," the Chorus says. But to Electra it seems immediately that the hair resembles hers, and the Chorus suggests that it might be "a secret gift from Orestes." Electra concludes: "He sent this severed strand, to do my father grace." She then launches into a monologue suspended on the thread of hope and knowledge: if only that curl "had the kind voice of a messenger so that my mind would not be torn in two," she exclaims. And as, distraught, she continues to examine the hair, she notices the footprints: they are two different feet, "of the man who gave his hair, and one who shared the road with him." She calls this "another sign," observing "heelmarks and the space between his heel and toe are like the prints I make." Anxious and disturbed, Electra stops: at the very moment when Orestes, followed by Pylades, comes toward her.

It's an extraordinary scene, and, immediately famous, it was rewritten, as we'll see, by Euripides and Sophocles, alluded to by Plato in the *Theaetetus*, where he speaks, precisely, of "footprints" and "recognition," and, finally, consecrated by Aristotle in the *Poetics* as the paradigm of a type of *anagnórisis*, that is, recognition, the kind that he called "through syllogism," or reasoning: Electra reasons that someone has arrived who is like her, but no one is the same except Orestes, therefore it's he who has arrived. A deduction, based on two "signs" (the lock of hair and the print) that the Electra of Aeschylus mentions, showing the playwright's great faith in the capacity of reason.

Aeschylus, though, is a writer too refined not to know that in such a scene reason has to be accompanied by emotion. He gives voice, then, to Electra's doubts ("if it had the kind voice of a messenger") and, when Orestes appears, presents a wonderful dialogue between brother and sister, with the display of the final proof: a cloak woven by Electra herself in which an animal design figures, symbol of the house of Atreus. The dialogue culminates in the short speech in which Orestes convinces Electra that he is really he:

You see my actual self and are slow to learn. And yet
you saw this strand of hair I cut in sign of grief
and shuddered with excitement, for you thought you saw
me, and again when you were measuring my tracks.
Now lay the severed strand against where it was cut
and see how well your brother's hair matches my head.
Look at this piece of weaving, the work of your hand,
with its blade strokes and figured design of beasts. No, no,
control yourself, and do not lose your head for joy.
I know those nearest to us hate us bitterly.

Finally, brother and sister can celebrate the reunion in what is from now on the "duet of recognition." Aeschylus' version not only stages the outburst of emotions but praises the re-formation of the *dómos*, the father's house: "the eagle's children."

This scene of recognition constitutes the only relief in the entire *Oresteia* until the final release: knowledge and fraternal love against hatred and Athys. Knowledge that is not abstract but physical: Electra calls Orestes father, mother, brother, and addresses him: "dearest treasured darling of my father's house, hope of the seed of our salvation, wept for." But it's a brief interlude. Orestes knows, and declares openly a little later, that he has to carry out his revenge: kill his mother and Aegisthus. The Chorus knows it, too, saying:

Right's anvil stands staunch on the ground
and the smith, Destiny, hammers out the sword.
Delayed in glory, pensive from
the murk, Vengeance brings home at last
a child, to wipe out the stain of blood shed long ago.

And so Orestes kills Aegisthus and then his mother, despite her sharp protests. Immediately, the "bloodhounds of my mother's hate," the Furies, begin to pursue him. Orestes flees, to the temple of Apollo in Delphi, where the god assures him protection and support, and then to the temple of Pallas Athena on the Acropolis in Athens, where the Furies have won a hearing with the goddess, and Orestes begs her to judge him fairly.

The move is decisive, because Athena is the goddess of knowledge and reason, and because she is the supreme protector of Athens, the city where Aeschylus lived, the city that had won the Persian wars (Aeschylus himself fought at Marathon, Salamis, and Platea) and was the cradle of democracy and the capital of Pericles and Greek culture. Athena decides to establish a court for crimes of blood in the Areopagus. At the same time, she announces the principles by which enforcement of the new law will be inspired: "respect for the citizens and the related fear," because without fear no justice will endure. Athena goes on to identify the ideal state: "no anarchy, no rule of a single master," the goddess says:

If it please you, men of Attica, hear my decree
now, on this first case of bloodletting I have judged.
For Aegeus' population, this forevermore
Shall be the ground where justices deliberate.
Here is the Hill of Ares, here the Amazons
encamped and built their shelters when they came in arms
for spite of Theseus, here they piled their rival towers
to rise, new city, and dare his city long ago,
and slew their beasts for Ares. So this rock is named
from then the Hill of Ares. Here the reverence
of citizens, their fear and kindred do-no-wrong
shall hold by day and in the blessing of night alike
all while the people do not muddy their own laws
with foul infusions. But if bright water you stain
with mud, you nevermore will find it fit to drink.
No anarchy, no rule of a single master. Thus
I advise my citizens to govern and to grace,
and not to cast fear utterly from your city. What
man who fears nothing at all is ever righteous? Such
be your just terrors, and you may deserve and have
salvation for your citadel, your land's defense,
such as is nowhere else found among men, neither
among the Scythians, nor the land that Pelops held.
I establish this tribunal. It shall be untouched
by money-making, grave but quick to wrath, watchful
to protect those who sleep, a sentry on the land.

These words I have unreeled are for my citizens,
advice into the future. All must stand upright
now, take each man his ballot in his hand, think on
his oath, and make his judgment. For my word is said.

Here in the place where, centuries later, the Apostle Paul
preached, and all but a few of his listeners abandoned him,
the last part of the *Oresteia* takes place. It's an actual trial:
Orestes is charged with matricide, the Furies are the accus-
ers, Apollo the witness. The debate ranges widely, taking in
the murder of Agamemnon and therefore all the action of
the play. At the end, Athena invites the judges to vote. The
result is a tie between those favorable to Orestes and those
opposed. Then Athena, who, as supreme judge and presi-
dent of the court, has rights of her own, takes advantage of
this and votes for Orestes: who is absolved. Athena also finds
a new home and new tasks for the Furies: given a new name,
the Eumenides, they will be honored in Athens and become
its protectors.

Thus the Oresteia sanctions the moment in which the Law
replaces the justice of retaliation and revenge, dominated by
Moira and Athys: a trial in court, where a human tribunal,
made up of real jurors, listens to the accused, the charge, the
witnesses, and votes according to its own convictions—a fun-
damental advance in civilization. This certainly won't prevent
tragedies of blood, but it will govern their outcomes, eliminat-
ing, at least in intention, the obligation to violence.

The "conclusion" of the *Oresteia* doesn't resolve the
problems that bind tragedy and justice. There is at least

one fundamental problem remaining. Who establishes the laws? And are we obliged to respect them, even when they appear to be or are unjust? Later, in Chapter VII, we'll examine the trial and death of Socrates: historically, the great fifth century of Athens ends there, in 399 B.C., with the death sentence and execution of the philosopher, who convinces Crito, in Plato's famous dialogue, that laws must be obeyed, even when they are applied by a court wrongly or unjustly. Some forty years earlier, however, the second of the great Greek tragedians, Sophocles, had staged, as part of a "Theban" trilogy, *Antigone*, which is devoted to the more "intimate" problem of justice.

Oedipus, the king of Thebes, is revealed to be the cause of the plague that rages in the city, because he killed his father, Laius, without knowing it, and, without knowing it, slept with his mother, Jocasta. Blinding himself, Oedipus has wandered through Greece with his daughters, Antigone and Ismene, and then "died" at Colonus, not far from Athens. The sons of Oedipus, Eteocles and Polynices, are fighting with one another to become ruler of Thebes, and all the Greek heroes of the time take part in this fratricidal war: Tydeus, the father of Diomedes, Melanippus, Capaneus, Amphiareus, Parthenopeus, and others. Aeschylus staged this story in *The Seven Against Thebes*, and it was later told in Latin hexameters by Statius.

During the war, Polynices and Eteocles kill each other, and Creon, Jocasta's brother, becomes the ruler of Thebes. He apparently intends to give burial to Eteocles, but to leave the corpse of Polynices unburied, prey to dogs and birds. Creon decrees that anyone who buries Polynices will be put to death. But Antigone wants to bury that brother, too, in spite of the new king's ban. And she proceeds, maintaining that there is a law higher than Creon's, or the state's: the law, both divine and human, of pity—the body must be buried. A sister must bury the body of a brother, if she is the only one left.

This is the origin of the dispute between Creon and Antigone, which is immediately transformed into open conflict when Antigone, who has tried to bury Polynices, is arrested. Again the conflict turns on justice, between the *nómos* proclaimed by an authority and the law that Antigone claims is higher, truer, and more just: the *ágrapta nómina*, the unwritten laws of the gods.

The debate over which of these two types of justice should prevail lasts at least up to Hegel—who had valuable things to say about *Antigone*—and beyond, through the authoritarian states of the twentieth century. Is it just, for example, to obey the laws of the state if those laws, including the inhuman ones regarding the extermination of the Jews, are proclaimed by the government of the Nazi party, or is it more just to rebel and to act according to our own conscience and nature as human beings, with the *pietas* inspired by the gods? Here is the reasoning of Antigone, in conversation with Creon:

CREON (to ANTIGONE):
>   Well, what do you say—you, hiding your head there: Do you admit, or do you deny the deed?
ANTIGONE:
>   I do admit it. I do not deny it.

CREON:

    Now tell me, in as few words as you can, Did you know the order
    forbidding such an act?

ANTIGONE:

    I knew it, naturally. It was plain enough.

CREON:

    And yet you dared to contravene it?

ANTIGONE:

    Yes. That order did not come from God. Justice,
    That dwells with the gods below, knows no such law.
    I did not think your edicts strong enough
    To overrule the unwritten unalterable laws
    Of God and heaven, you being only a man.
    They are not of yesterday or to-day, but everlasting,
    Though where they came from, none of us can tell.
    Guilty of their transgression before God
    I cannot be, for any man on earth.
    I knew that I should have to die, of course,
    With or without your order. If it be soon,
    So much the better. Living in daily torment
    As I do, who would not be glad to die?
    This punishment will not be any pain.
    Only if I had let my mother's son
    Lie there unburied, then I could not have borne it.
    This I can bear. Does that seem foolish to you?
    Or is it you that are foolish to judge me so?[25]

From this moment on, Antigone becomes the example of the defender of the laws that are more profoundly divine, and therefore more human. Those, precisely, with which we must always reckon, even if the law of the state proclaims the contrary.

A play by Sophocles is never so simple, however—neither its plot nor its themes. This is not the place to examine the latter, whose many facets make the play appear much less monolithic. But the action, too, unfolds with abrupt reversals right at the end.

Creon spares the life of Antigone, and has her locked up in a cave so that she will die there. But Antigone is the betrothed of Haemon, Creon's own son, and Haemon tries to intervene with his father to free the prisoner. Creon is unbending, but shortly afterward he receives a visit from Tiresias, who asserts that Thebes is contaminated by an "illness" coming from the unburied corpse of Polynices. The king sends Tiresias away, cursing him, and accusing him of wanting to take advantage of the situation, but he orders that Polynices be buried and Antigone freed.

Everything would be fine and the play would have a happy ending if two messengers didn't bring other news: Antigone, fearing that she would spend the rest of her life in the cave, has killed herself. Haemon has followed her, and so, too, has Eurydice, Creon's wife. In despair she concludes: "Come, my last hour and fairest, My only happiness . . . come soon. Let me not see another day." Creon, who at the end says, "I am nothing. I have no life," has paid for his tyrannical presumption: the unjust decree of a man can't replace the unwritten laws of the gods.

VI
THE TRAGEDY OF KNOWLEDGE

O divinity of sky, and swift-winged winds, and leaping streams,
O countless laughter of the sea's waves,
O Earth, mother of all life!
On you, and on the all-seeing circle of the sun, I call:
See what is done by gods to me, a god!
See with what outrage
Racked and tortured
I am to agonize
For a thousand years! . . .
For bestowing gifts upon mankind
I am harnessed in this torturing clamp. For I am he
Who hunted out the source of fire, and stole it, packed
In pith of a dry fennel-stalk. And fire has proved
For men a teacher in every art, their grand resource.
That was the sin for which I now pay the full price,
Bared to the winds of heaven, bound and crucified.

For the Greeks, human knowledge originates in an act of presumption but also of generosity and compassion: the Titan Prometheus' gift of fire to human beings. It's an act of presumption and overreach, because a god shouldn't have taken pity on humans, who are infinitely inferior to the heavenly beings, and bestowed on them a divine privilege. That's why Prometheus is condemned by Zeus to be chained forever to a rock beside the sea and, later, to endure an eagle gnawing his liver. Aeschylus presents him like that, in the first scene of *Prometheus Bound*. Knowledge is forbidden to man, somewhat as in the Book of Genesis, where God forbids Adam and Eve to eat the fruit of the tree of the knowledge of good and evil.

In spite of the numerous hypotheses proposed by scholars, we don't know exactly what the Bible means by "the knowledge of good and evil." We do know precisely what Prometheus intended to do by giving fire to men. He says it himself, describing the sufferings of human beings, who, before he gave them "mind and reason," were children:

In those days they had eyes, but sight was meaningless;
Heard sounds, but could not listen; all their length of life
They passed like shapes in dreams, confused and purposeless.
Of brick-built, sun-warmed houses, or of carpentry,
They had no notion; lived in holes like swarms of ants.

Men were ignorant of everything: numbers, letters, astronomy, domestication of animals, navigation, medicine, divination, and even mining minerals. Primitive humanity, a child in everything and for everything, dimwitted, truly the troglodyte shadow of a dream that lives haphazardly, owes its knowledge of all these things to Prometheus. Plato also records this in the *Protagoras*, where he has the father of the Sophists, around a decade older than Socrates, make this claim:

Thus did Epimetheus, who, not being very wise, forget that he had distributed among the brute animals all the qualities which he had to give—and when he came to man, who was still unprovided, he was terribly perplexed. Now while he was in this perplexity, Prometheus came to inspect the distribution, and he found that the other animals were suitably furnished, but that man alone was naked and shoeless, and had neither bed nor arms of defence. The appointed hour was approaching when man in his turn was to go forth into the light of day; and Prometheus, not knowing how he could devise his salvation, stole the mechanical arts of Hephaestus and Athene, and fire with them (they could neither have been acquired nor used without fire), and gave them to man. Thus man had the wisdom necessary to the support of life, but political wisdom he had not; for that was in the keeping of Zeus, and the power of Prometheus did not extend to entering into the citadel of heaven, where Zeus dwelt . . . but he did enter by stealth into the common workshop of Athene and Hephaestus, in which they used to practise their favourite arts, and carried off Hephaestus' art of working by fire, and also the art of Athene, and gave them to man. And in this way man was supplied with the means of life. But Prometheus is said to have been afterwards prosecuted for theft . . . Now man, having a share of the divine attributes, was at first the only one of the animals who had any gods, because he alone was of their kindred; and he would raise altars and images of them. He was not long in inventing articulate speech and names; and he also constructed houses and clothes and shoes and beds, and drew sustenance from the earth.[26]

There must have been a very lively debate about what knowledge primitive man had and how he gained it— whether by divine gift or the development of innate faculties—in fifth-century Greece. For Anaxagoras, hands were the essential tool, and man was distinguished from the animals by his capacity to use experience, memory, knowledge, and technique. Aristotle and Galen objected that it was more reasonable to think that man has hands because he is the wisest of the living creatures, rather than the contrary, whereas Democritus claimed that men were disciples of the animals, because in the most important arts they are imitators: "of the spider in weaving and mending, of the swallows in constructing houses, of the songbirds, the swan, and the nightingale in song." Plutarch, however, citing the same passage, exclaims: "We are quite ridiculous when we celebrate the beasts as models for our capacity to learn."

Democritus' *Little World System* presents an articulate and reasoned history of primitive man, in which the turning point is represented by the discovery of fire and the central motivation for development is, first, necessity, and then the increase in desires that comes with the increase in comforts. Lucretius, inspired by Epicurus, provides a grand portrait of human evolution in Book V of *De rerum natura*.

Sophocles and Euripides are the playwrights who, along with Aeschylus, in *Prometheus*, join the discussion. In Sophocles' *Antigone* the Chorus enthusiastically celebrates man, the "greatest wonder" on earth, and his autonomy. It's one of the most famous hymns of the age of Pericles:

Wonders are many on earth, and the greatest of these
Is man, who rides the ocean and takes his way
Through the deeps, through wind-swept valleys of perilous seas
 That surge and sway.
He is master of ageless Earth, to his own will bending
The immortal mother of gods by the sweat of his brow,
As year succeeds to year, with toil unending
 Of mule and plough.
He is lord of all things living; birds of the air,
Beasts of the field, all creatures of sea and land
He taketh, cunning to capture and ensnare

　　With sleight of hand;
Hunting the savage beast from the upland rocks,
Taming the mountain monarch in his lair,
Teaching the wild horse and the roaming ox
　　His yoke to bear.
The use of language, the wind-swift motion of brain
He learnt; found out the laws of living together
In cities, building him shelter against the rain
　　And wintry weather.
There is nothing beyond his power. His subtlety
Meeteth all chance, all danger conquereth.
For every ill he hath found its remedy,
　　Save only death.
O wondrous subtlety of man, that draws
To good or evil ways! Great honour is given
And power to him who upholdeth his country's laws
　　And the justice of heaven.
But he that, too rashly daring, walks in sin
In solitary pride to his life's end.
At door of mine shall never enter in
To call me friend.

In Euripides' *Suppliants* Theseus returns, instead, to the action of the divine:

I thank the god who has put order into our disordered and wild lives.

　　That god has put reason into our thoughts and words into mouths, so that we can understand each other. Then he has given us the fruit of the soil to eat and with that fruit he gave us the heavenly rain drops that nourishes that fruit and quenches the thirst of our bellies.

　　As well as all that, the same god has taught us how to set up fortresses against the Winter's attacks of icy cold and the sun's blaze of Summer.

He taught us how to sail the oceans and make trade with other nations so that each nation can obtain what it lacks.[27]

Whether human civilization originated as a divine gift and impulse or as a result of qualities innate in man himself is not an idle question: it means asking whether mankind is entirely dependent or autonomous, and giving a mythic-religious answer or a scientific one to the problems of the Beginning that plague us. A Beginning that, I would note, stands halfway between the "material" one that the pre-Socratic thinkers, as we've seen, seek in the cosmos and the absolute—indeed, metaphysical—origin of knowledge investigated by Aristotle. In the reconstructions of this process that I've just outlined, there is no mention of the wonder that inspires the questions of the child humanity and impels it to "philosophize": not even in the Plato of the *Protagoras*, although in the *Theaetetus* he had claimed that philosophy originated in wonder; or in Anaxagoras, so passionate about investigation and contemplation of the stars. In fact, what the Greeks establish is a *historical anthropology* of great breadth and depth, which has many points of contact with the anthropology conceived by the moderns.

Aeschylus' *Prometheus* offers a mythic and poetic version of this episode that has great evocative power. The very figure of the chained Titan, who laments and protests violently against the will of Zeus, has become an icon of the imagination. Prometheus feels pity only for his brother Atlas, condemned to stand upright in the far west, holding up on his shoulders the pillar of the sky and the earth; and for the monster Typheus, who rebelled against all the gods and was crushed under Etna. Prometheus himself is a rebel against the Olympic order, and a hero of knowledge: he "thinks first" (that is the meaning of his name), knows how to send his mind forward, to fore-see. The day will come, he understands, when he will be freed. And yet he knows that that moment has not yet arrived, that *móira,* which "brings everything to fulfillment," isn't ready: that skill, the *téchne* of which he is the master, is "weaker" than *anánche*, Necessity. Against the insuperable wall of destiny intelligence is of no avail—nothing avails, not even the immense power of Zeus. We'll see, in the story of Oedipus, a demonstration of the impotence of intelligence, but perhaps it would be useful to pause for a moment to consider what type of human knowledge is possible for a tragic poet like Aeschylus.

We can learn by reading *Agamemnon*, the first of the three plays of the *Oresteia*. At a certain point in the play the Chorus sings the famous Hymn to Zeus, in which the supreme divinity of the Greek pantheon is invoked by name alone to indicate the highest and most powerful God in the world:

Zeus: whatever he may be, if this name
pleases him in invocation,
thus I call upon him.
I have pondered everything
yet I cannot find a way,
only Zeus, to cast this dead weight of ignorance
finally from out my brain . . .

Cry aloud without fear the victory of Zeus,
You will not have failed the truth:

Zeus who guided men to think,
who has laid it down that wisdom comes alone through suffering.
still there drips in sleep against the heart
grief of memory; against
our pleasure we are temperate
from the gods who sit in grandeur
grace comes somehow violent.

Suffering, then, is a prerequisite for wisdom. If the Jewish Genesis postulates that the price of wisdom is death, the Greeks knew perfectly well that wisdom can be acquired only through suffering. It was common knowledge from the times of Homer and Hesiod, but it was really Aeschylus, at the beginning of tragedy, who expressed it memorably.

Páthei máthos: this is Zeus' expression for human *phronéin*, the "prudence" that is wisdom and knowledge. An anguish that recalls sufferings: an immense *sorrow* that oppresses the human heart and represents the very source of knowledge.

Wisdom through suffering. Man has no wisdom that doesn't come through suffering. The ultimate embodiment of this, proof that it is impossible for human intelligence to conquer destiny, is Oedipus. Thanks precisely to his wisdom and his intelligence, Oedipus has defeated the Sphinx, guessing the solution to the riddle she presents: what is the animal that as a child walks on four legs, as an adult on two, and in old age, leaning on a stick, on three? Man, naturally:

he's always there, at the center of everything. For getting rid of the Sphinx, Oedipus is rewarded with absolute rule over Thebes and the honor of marrying Jocasta, the widow of the old lord, Laius. The plague is raging in the city, and Oedipus has sent his brother-in-law Creon to Delphi to consult the oracle and discover what should be done to eradicate it. The oracle replies that the cause of the *míasma*, the infection, is the presence of an impure being: of the man who is guilty of killing Laius. Oedipus is the champion of knowledge: and so he takes on the task of discovering the guilty man, and through a detailed investigation, with startling revelations, he finally comes to a conclusion.

The first phase of the investigation consists of interrogating Tiresias, the seer-prophet we have already encountered in the *Odyssey*. Tiresias is the repository of a knowledge that is not rational, not logical; it has nothing to do with the knowledge of Oedipus but is much older. At first obliquely, then more and more directly, Tiresias accuses Oedipus of the murder of Laius. Furious, Oedipus drives him out of Thebes, accusing him of plotting with Creon to seize power. In a later conversation with Creon, he repeats the accusation and announces that he will condemn him to death; then, under pressure from the Chorus, he decides on exile.

The second stage of the investigation is the encounter with Jocasta. She reveals that according to a prophecy Laius would be killed by a son: instead he was killed "by outland robbers / At a place where three roads meet." Nevertheless, when a son was born, Laius had the infant's feet tied together, and "he cast it out / (By other hands, not his) with rivetted ankles / To perish on the empty mountain-side."

The oracle was therefore mistaken. But Oedipus is disturbed: he asks where the murder took place, how much time has passed since then, what Laius looked like, if he traveled modestly or had an escort—in short, he asks all the circumstantial questions that a detective would. He becomes increasingly distressed by Jocasta's answers, until he asks if it would be possible to summon the man who told the story to Jocasta herself. He says then that he is the son of Polybus and Meropé, the rulers of Corinth. One day, a man who'd been drinking said he was not the true son of his father; Oedipus asked his parents for an explanation, but then wanted to question the oracle of Delphi about it. Apollo, he says, didn't deign to respond, but predicted that he would sleep with his mother and kill his father. So he left Corinth forever and fled where he would never meet his father and mother. In the place mentioned by Jocasta, just at the convergence of three roads, he encountered an old man in a horse-drawn carriage with an appearance similar to her description, accompanied by a herald. The two pushed him violently off the road, Oedipus reacted, the old man struck him with the whip, Oedipus in an impulse of rage attacked him with the stick, knocking him to the ground, and then killed the herald, too. It is therefore crucial for Oedipus to question the shepherd who witnessed this event, to find out if Laius was killed by "robbers" or by one man alone. In the first case, he, Oedipus, would be innocent; in the second guilty.

The surprise arrives quickly. A messenger from Corinth brings the news that the people there are about to elect Oedipus king of the region of the Isthmus: Polybus is dead.

While Oedipus agrees with Jocasta that oracles have no value, since he didn't kill Polybus, he declares that he doesn't want to go to Corinth, for fear of "pollution through his parents." But the messenger replies that Polybus and Meropé were not his real parents, and that he himself delivered him to them as an infant, freeing his "rivetted ankles," from which his name derives ("Oidipous" comes from "knowing," *óida*, and "foot," *pous*). The child had been given to him, he adds, when Oedipus questions him further, by another shepherd, "one of Laius' men." Jocasta, he concludes, could confirm everything. But Jocasta has understood: while Oedipus proclaims that nothing will keep him from learning the truth and finding out his origin and his lineage (*génos* and/or *spérma*). Jocasta shouts at him, "Doomed man! O never live to learn the truth!" and goes back alone into the palace. Oedipus then proclaims a real act of faith in himself:

Let all come out,
However vile! However base it be,
I must unlock the secret of my birth [*spérma*].
The woman, with more than woman's pride, is shamed
By my low origin. I am the child of Fortune,
The giver of good, and I shall not be shamed.
She is my mother; my sisters are the Seasons;
My rising and my falling march with theirs.
Born thus, I ask to be no other man
Than that I am, and *will know who I am* [*génos*].

Soon afterward the Theban shepherd who had given the child to the Corinthian shepherd arrives. Subjected to Oedipus' stringent interrogation, and threatened with torture, he has to admit that he took the child from

Jocasta with the order to kill him because of the old prophecy that otherwise he would kill his father. The inquiry is complete: the detective himself is guilty: "Alas!" Oedipus exclaims. "All out! All known, no more concealment! O Light! May I never look on you again, Revealed as I am, sinful in my begetting, Sinful in marriage, sinful in shedding of blood!"

As a mystery novel, as the reconstruction of a crime that is patricide and incest, Sophocles' *Oedipus the King* is fantastic: perhaps the best mystery novel ever written, with a clocklike mechanism that doesn't let up until the sensational final reversal. Oedipus wants to know his *génos,* but, when he finds out, he discovers that he is the son of a man he killed and of a woman with whom he has slept and produced children. The knowledge that he has acquired turns out to be a tragedy. And Oedipus blinds himself, so that he can no longer see the world in which he has committed so much evil.

The problem for us moderns lies in an essential question: is Oedipus guilty of these horrors? In the next play of the Theban series, *Oedipus at Colonus*, he himself maintains that he didn't know, and so is not guilty. Every event was imposed on him by the combination of Fate and Tyche, destiny. For the Greeks, Oedipus is, in fact, guilty, but no more and no less than every human being. Because every human being is subject to *fallibility*: not to individual guilt in the Christian sense, and therefore not to sin, but to the possibility of erring and falling: fallibility. Oedipus has committed a *hamartía*, that is, a guilty error. But the word *hamartía*, which in classical Greek means "error," in the Greek of the Christians means "sin."

Between the two concepts there's quite a difference: we commit a sin knowingly (as when Adam and Eve eat the fruit that was expressly forbidden by God), while we can commit a guilty act without being aware of it or ultimately responsible. Oedipus didn't know that the man he killed was his father, or that the woman he married was his mother, and in fact he had done everything possible to avoid both things. Yet Oedipus is guilty, profoundly guilty, as are all human beings. We could say that an "original guilt" weighs on him—I don't want to say "original sin," to avoid confusion with a different setting—an original guilt that concerns us all. We all want to know our origins, our *spérma* and our *génos* by means of reason and knowledge: all of us who stole fire along with Prometheus, or received it from him.

And to think that Sophocles, who, by means of an extraordinary dramatic mechanism, so brilliantly describes this plunge of knowledge into nothing—that it was Sophocles, along with Aeschylus, but in a different way, who celebrated knowledge. In the series of plays about Electra, all inspired by Aeschylus' *Libation Bearers*, Sophocles' *Electra*, which comes third, after that of Euripides, seems to forcefully reiterate faith in reason. In *The Libation Bearers* we encounter the recognition scene that I discussed in the previous chapter. At the tomb of her father, Agamemnon, Electra finds a lock of hair, holds it next to her hair, and observes: "But this hair is like mine." She then elaborates what Aristotle, in the *Poetics*, calls *syllogismós*, a syllogism: she reasons deductively. "This lock of hair is like mine, no one can have hair like mine except my brother Orestes, so Orestes is here." The same thing happens shortly afterward with the footprint that Electra notices on the ground, a scene that Plato recalls in the *Theaetetus* when he speaks of the process of knowledge as recognition of a sign already written in memory. Again Electra develops a *syllogismós:* "Here is a footprint, my foot is similar to it, no one can have feet like mine except Orestes, so Orestes has come."

It's an emotional moment, in which Electra begins to reason like Sherlock Holmes—in short, like a detective in our modern world who deduces from the evidence, from the clues she's found: the lock of hair and the footprint. The two arguments that Electra unfolds starting from those clues are not sufficient, as she herself recognizes, to prove definitively that Orestes is present, but they indicate that, using reason, the human mind can make a good part of the journey necessary for the acquisition of knowledge: in substance, they declare that the playwright Aeschylus believes in reason.

Yet this scene was immediately challenged by Euripides, who inserts in his *Electra* an episode that rewrites Aeschylus. In the Euripidean drama an old teacher comes to Electra (she has married a farmer) and announces: "I went to your father's tomb, I found a lock of hair that is exactly like yours, and so it must have been Orestes who left it." In other words the old man repeats the syllogism of Aeschylus' *Electra*. But Euripides' Electra has been to school with the Sophists, and replies: "But please, have you ever seen the hair of a woman and the hair of a man? They have no relation: they are completely different! And then you say 'footprint,' but the footprint of a woman is smaller than a man's. How can they be the same?" Euripides is cheating, because Aeschylus didn't use the word "equal" (*hísos*); he said "in proportion to" (*sýmmetros*). But, in essence, Euripides' Electra has fun attacking and destroying Aeschylus' reasoning: or, rather, deconstructing the contextual proofs that would establish that reasoning as valid. The inevitable conclusion is that we can't acquire rational, deductive knowledge of the presence of Orestes.

But there is a scene of recognition between Orestes and Electra in Euripides' *Electra* that follows a tested Homeric model: the scar that Orestes has on his forehead and that he got playing as a child. That scar is the tragedy's version of the one that Odysseus has on his thigh, by means of which the old nurse Euryclea recognizes him. On this "sign" both the teacher and Electra agree. It's very likely that Euripides intended this change with respect to the Aeschylian scene to signal his skepticism toward the faith in rationalism demonstrated by his older colleague.

Then comes the *Electra* of Sophocles, the playwright who composed and presented *Oedipus the King* and is now eighty. In his version of the play, Sophocles divides the recognition scene in two. In the first, an old teacher brings Electra and Clytemnestra the news that Orestes has died during a horse race in the Delphic Games. The urn that contains his ashes will soon be brought to them by Pylades. Shortly afterward, Electra's sister, Chrysothemis, reports that she went to the tomb of Agamemnon and found a lock of hair there:

All was quiet.
So I crept nearer to the tomb; and there at its edge
I found a lock of hair, newly cut off.
And O, when I saw it, at once my heart was filled
With the thought of my best beloved, my own Orestes.
I took it up in my hands, in reverent silence,
But weeping for joy, knowing, as I knew at once,
That no one else could have brought that offering.
Who else should do such a thing but you or I?
I know it was not I; nor you—how could you,
When you are strictly forbidden to leave the house
Even for worship? Nor is it the kind of thing
Our mother likes to do, or if she did
Could do without our knowledge.[28]

This passage of intense emotion is Sophocles' first response to the problem of Aeschylus and Euripides. Sophocles, too, uses the lock of hair and has Chrysothemis consider it proof: not by means of the rational argument that it is similar to her own hair but, rather, by a subtle, mysterious process of memory and the association of ideas. A sudden light invades Chrysothemis' soul: the image-thought of seeing a sign of Orestes. For a moment there is no trace of rationality: Chrysothemis picks up the lock of hair as if to appropriate the sign for herself, to touch with her hand the evidence of her own feelings and her own thoughts, and, surrounded by silence, she bursts into tears. As far as she's concerned, the recognition is complete.

The *syllogismós* belongs to the present, a rationalization that succeeds an intuitive process. Now, one can reason by exclusion: if it wasn't me, or you, or our mother, then it must be Orestes. After Euripides' criticism, Sophocles completely eliminates the concept of resemblance that was the basis of the Aeschylian syllogism, but insists nevertheless on the value of reasoning, stating implicitly that it is possible and that in fact it derives directly, in the human mind, from the apprehension of reality by means of intuition dominated by emotion.

In fact the resolution takes place during the same scene and includes a double recognition. Orestes, disguised, brings the urn to Electra, and she takes it in her hands and utters a moving lament over it. While her last words are covered by the philosophical consolation of the Chorus, Orestes feels he can't continue to pretend and acknowledges his sister: "What can I say? God help me, what can I say? Silence will stifle me . . . You are the lady Electra, are you not?" The dialogue develops rapidly. Electra notes that her interlocutor is the only one who pities her, and Orestes responds: "No other man has ever come that knew your sorrows as his own." Electra thinks he might be a distant relative. Orestes then decides to tell her everything. That the urn contains the ashes of Orestes is a fiction. That the young man's grave doesn't exist, since the living don't have graves. The enigma is solved in the recognition:

ELECTRA:
    He lives?
ORESTES:
    As I live.
ELECTRA:
    Is it really you?
ORESTES:
    Look—father's signet—do you believe me now?

ELECTRA:
  O light! O joy!
ORESTES:
  I share it.
ELECTRA:
  Is this indeed
  Your voice again?
ORESTES:
  Ask for no other witness.
ELECTRA:
  Your hand in mine?
ORESTES:
  For ever.
ELECTRA:
  Women, women!
  It is Orestes, look, women of Argos!
  His death was only a trick, and by that trick
  He has been given back to us!

The final act of recognition, therefore, consists in what Aristotle would call an "external sign," the ring belonging to Orestes' father, Agamemnon, which conclusively proves his identity. Yet recognition itself would be impossible without the two key lines, "All that I see speaks of your load of hardship," and "No other man has ever come that knew your sorrows as his own." What these two lines mean is that Orestes recognizes Electra because of her sufferings, and she has to recognize him because he shares them. In other words, recognition sinks its roots into the common experience of *páschein*: suffering, pain, sorrow. As if to say, knowledge is obtained by suffering: *páthei máthos*. The supreme example of that is, precisely, Oedipus, whose rational knowledge shatters against the wall of chance and

destiny in *Oedipus the King*. When, in the final drama of
the ninety-year-old Sophocles, *Oedipus at Colonus*, an old,
blind Oedipus, accompanied by Antigone and immediately
joined by Ismene, arrives in the village of Colonus, just out-
side Athens, his sufferings have redeemed him. He has
come to die, as Socrates will soon. He no longer has a need
for investigations carried out by reason, and speaks in the
prophetic tones of Tiresias: he knows with certainty, he
says, that the time has come, here and now.

VII
DEATH AND LOGOS

Please consider my object in telling you this. I want to explain to you how the attack on my reputation first started. When I heard about the oracle's answer, I said to myself, "What is the god saying, and what is his hidden meaning? I am only too conscious that I have no claim to wisdom, great or small; so what can he mean by asserting that I am the wisest man in the world? He cannot be telling a lie; that would not be right for him."

After puzzling about it for some time, I set myself at last with considerable reluctance to check the truth of it in the following way. I went to interview a man with a high reputation for wisdom, because I felt that here if anywhere I should succeed in disproving the oracle and pointing out to my divine authority, "You said that I was the wisest of men, but here is a man who is wiser than I am."

Well, I gave a thorough examination to this person—I need not mention his name, but it was one of our politicians that I was studying when I had this experience—and in conversation with him I formed the impression that although in many people's opinion, and especially in his own, he appeared to be wise, in fact he was not. Then when I began to try to show him that he only thought he was wise and was not really so, my efforts were resented by him and by many of the other people present. However, I reflected as I walked away: "Well, I am certainly wiser than this man. It is only too likely that neither of us has any knowledge to boast of; but he thinks that he knows something which he does not know, whereas I am quite conscious of my ignorance. At any rate it seems that I am wiser than he is to this small extent, that I do not think that I know what I do not know.

After this I went on to interview a man with an even greater reputation for wisdom, and I formed the same impression again; and here too I incurred the resentment of the man himself and a number of others.[29]

Socrates stands before the judges of Athens accused of corrupting youth and attacking traditional religion. He wants to reconstruct the origin of such a charge, and concludes that it must come from the envy and incomprehension of his accusers. We're right in the middle of that remarkable piece of writing that is the *Apology of Socrates,* composed by one of his disciples, Plato. Socrates explains: he has received from Delphi not only the traditional message, "Know thyself," but also the oracular judgment that there is no one in Athens wiser than him. But he wants to understand how "the god" can utter such an oracle. The god can't lie, naturally, and so Socrates decides to "check the truth" of it, which consists in going around interrogating men who have the reputation of being wise. He consults experts in every subject, poets, and playwrights, and discovers that though they all believe they are wise, they are not, that he is wiser than they are, if only because he knows that he doesn't know. Socrates' investigation isn't well received: those he questions to verify their ignorance resent him. That explains the hostility toward him.

The trial of Socrates is a crucial moment in the history of the West, and its impact will be felt for the next twenty-five hundred years. In various ways it anticipates the trial of Jesus of Nazareth in the Gospels: as the latter marks the birth of Christianity, so the former marks the beginning of true philosophy, and is the highest testimony of an old thinker, a philosopher—that is, a lover of knowledge. Not the knowledge that addresses natural phenomena, the material "beginnings" of the cosmos, like that of the pre-Socratics, but, rather, as Aristotle posits in the *Metaphysics*, the knowledge that examines ethical questions, that is, man, and against the background of those investigates the universal. It's significant that that new investigation precipitates and solidifies into a trial, and thus touches on the problem of justice.

Because the problem, in the first place, is whether the trial of Socrates is fair or not, and if Socrates was right to agree to it and accept the death sentence that comes out of it. But what does a "fair" trial mean? And will Socrates have to obey the laws of Athens, even if he's found guilty, and even if he considers himself not guilty of the crimes he's accused of? These problems are at the heart of Plato's first dialogues, that is, the *Apology of Socrates* and the *Crito*. After Socrates has been sentenced, he is urged by his friends and disciples to leave Athens, to flee. If he fled, he would only be avoiding an unjust sentence. Other thinkers have taken this route: Anaxagoras, protected by Pericles, fled and saved his life. Not Socrates. Socrates remains in Athens and, in the *Apology* and then in the *Crito*, expounds on what it means to respect the laws. In the culminating passage of the *Crito* he imagines that as he is on the point of fleeing the laws appear before him and reproach him. "Suppose," he says to Crito, "while we were preparing to run away from here (or however one should describe it),"

the Laws and communal interest of Athens were to come and confront us with this question: "Now, Socrates, what are you proposing to do? Can you deny that by this act which you are contemplating you intend, so far as you have the power, to destroy us, the Laws, and the whole State as well? Do you imagine that a city can continue to exist and not be turned upside down, if the legal judgments which are pronounced in it have no force but are nullified and destroyed by private persons?"

There is, the laws continue, a pact between them and Socrates, which would be broken if he decided to flee. Furthermore, they brought him into the world, reared him, educated him: and they have clearly informed him, over time, that he is permitted, "if he is not satisfied with us, to take his property and go away wherever he likes." But if a person remains, then "he has in fact undertaken" to do what the laws tell him.

In short, there is a pact and a moral obligation to respect it, or the civic order is destroyed. Having accepted the legal framework of Athens, Socrates can't leave after the sentence. But there's more, and it's more fundamental. Socrates has publicly undertaken to die. He says it, with unusual force, before the judges who have just condemned him. Earlier, as if sketching the argument he will lay out to Crito, he ties death to respect for the law:

This being so, it would be shocking inconsistency on my part, gentlemen, if when the officers whom you chose to command me assigned me my position at Potidaea and Amphipolis and Delium, I remained at my post like anyone else and faced death, and yet afterwards, when God appointed me, as I supposed and believed, to the duty of leading the philosophic life, examining myself and others, I were then through fear of death or of any other danger to desert my post.

Then he moves conclusively to defend his choice to stay where he is and die. As soon as he is condemned to death, he explains that we should never fear death, and that "we are quite mistaken in supposing death to be an evil." Either death means annihilation, losing everything, falling into not being—he says—and then there's no reason to fear it, because "not being" means *not* being: not feeling anymore, not seeing anymore, not suffering anymore. Or death is, as tradition maintains, a descent to Hades, where we will find all those who have preceded us: our dead. We'll find not only those in our family but also our ancestors, the great men of the past, and we'll be able to converse with them; in fact, in the case of Socrates, he'll be able to go on examining people's minds, even after death, as he does in life. There's no need to fear death. How great is this teaching of Socrates! Who—note—is lecturing to the judges who have condemned him to death, and whom he compares, with sovereign disdain, to the "true" judges, like Rhadamanthus, Minos, Aeacus, and Triptolemus. And then wouldn't it be nice to linger with the figures of myth?

If, on the other hand, death is a removal from here to some other place, and if what we are told is true, that all the dead are there, what greater blessing could there be than this, gentlemen of the jury? If on arrival in the other world, beyond the reach of these so-called jurors here, one will find there the true jurors who are said to preside in those courts, Minos and Rhadamanthus and Aeacus and Triptolemus and all those other demigods who were upright in their earthly life, would that be an unrewarding place to settle? Put it in this way: how much would one of you give to meet Orpheus and Musaeus, Hesiod and Homer? I am willing to die ten times over if this account is true.

For me at least it would be a wonderful personal experience to join them there, to meet Palamedes and Ajax the son of Telamon and any other heroes of the old days who met their death through an unjust trial, and to compare my fortunes with theirs—it would be rather amusing, I think—and above all I should like to spend my time there, as here, in examining and searching people's minds, to find out who is really wise among them, and who only thinks that he is. What would one not give, gentlemen, to be able to scrutinize the leader of that great host against Troy, or Odysseus, or Sisyphus, or the thousands of other men and women whom one could mention? Their company and conversation—like the chance to examine them—would be unimaginable happiness. At any rate I presume that they do not put one to death there for such conduct; because apart from the other happiness in which their world surpasses ours, they are now immortal for the rest of time, if what we are told is true.

While Hesiod, the pre-Socratics, and the Plato of the *Timaeus* are concerned with the origins of the cosmos, Socrates confronts the end of man and sees it as a non-end. He resorts to archaic concepts of Hades, to the vision of myth and poetry—of Homer. He does it again at the end of the *Phaedo*, shortly before he dies, when, illustrating his idea of the universe, he lays out his concept of the other world. He looks at death with the eyes of the *imagination* and—a man who has been condemned for impiety and disdain for the old religion—with boundless trust in traditional beliefs. But Socrates hasn't finished yet. With unexpected urgency, he addresses the judges as human beings subject to death themselves:

You too, gentlemen of the jury, must look forward to death with confidence, and fix your minds on this one belief, which is certain:

that nothing can harm a good man either in life or after death, and his fortunes are not a matter of indifference to the gods. This present experience of mine does not result from mere earthly causes; I am quite clear that the time had come when it was better for me to die and be released from my distractions. That is why my sign never turned me back. For my own part I bear no grudge against all those who condemned me and accused me, although it was not with this kind intention that they did so, but because they thought that they were hurting me; and that is culpable of them. However, I ask them to grant me one favour. When my sons grow up, gentlemen, if you think that they are putting money or anything else before goodness, take your revenge by plaguing them as I plagued you; and if they fancy themselves for no reason, you must scold them just as I scolded you, for neglecting the important things and thinking that they are good for something when they are good for nothing. If you do this, I shall have had justice at your hands—I and my children.

Well, now it is time to be off, I to die and you to live; but which of us has the happier prospect is unknown to anyone but God.

A memorable phrase, which ends the *Apology* on an oracular note. In the next dialogue, *Crito*, which is set in prison, the problem again is, as we've seen, the law. It's essential to note, however, that both in the *Apology* and in the *Crito* we are witnessing the birth of dialectic: that is, the particular method of discussing a specific problem point by point, by means of reasoning (in the *Crito*, for example, respect for the law). One could even say that the dialectic method, used by Socrates in his entire practice as an itinerant, interrogating thinker (and already seen in the *Euthyphro*), is refined and deepened in the *Apology* and the *Crito*, as if, approaching death, the philosopher wanted to rely increasingly on *lógos*—logical, rational discourse—and gradually abandon the more traditional forms of mythic thought: that is, *mýthos*.

In the fourth Platonic dialogue, the *Phaedo*, the impression that dialectic has its origin in death becomes even stronger, because in the *Phaedo* Plato imagines that Socrates, about to drink the hemlock and die, proves, using logic, the immortality of the soul! But let's go in order. After the conversation with Crito, Socrates remains in prison. The *Phaedo* contains the account of Socrates' last hours that Phaedo, who is present, gives Echecrates. The moment of death approaches. As it arrives, Socrates spends some time explaining to Cebes why he has been composing poems adapted from Aesop's fables and the proem to Apollo, and then why the philosopher avoids suicide yet welcomes death. It frees man from his body and is thus the culmination of a life spent in search of knowledge, because the body is a hindrance to the philosopher in his attempt to understand the Forms of things.

An increasingly Platonic Socrates (because of an illness, Plato isn't physically present) now launches into three demonstrations—the argument from opposites, the theory of recollection, and the argument from affinities— concerning the existence of a life after death, the nature of the universe, and the immortality of the soul. Socrates echoes, and sometimes mocks, the theories of Empedocles, Anaximenes, and Heraclitus, approves some of the ideas of his older contemporary Anaxagoras, and, as the character who spoke in the *Apology*, uses mythic and even Orphic stories about the beyond. Many names of rivers and other features of the world beyond that are found in poetry, especially the *Odyssey,* are mentioned here—Tartarus, Ocean, Acheron, Styx, Pyriphlegethon, and Cocytus.

The newly dead, Socrates maintains, are judged immediately after the crossing and sent to their appropriate destinations. Those who have lived neutral lives are sent to Acheron and, after crossing it, to the Acherusian Lake, where they remain to purify themselves. Those who have committed inexpiable sins are thrown into the depths of Tartarus, "from whence they emerge no more." Human beings who "are judged to have lived a life of surpassing holiness" have permission to live on the earth's surface, while those who have purified themselves through philosophy will live without bodies and reach habitations of ineffable beauty. "Of course," Socrates adds, "no reasonable man ought to insist that the facts are exactly as I have described them. But that either this or something very like it is a true account of our souls" and their habitations, since it has been proved that the soul is immortal—that is indeed appropriate, and is also a belief that's worth the risk, and the risk is noble: "We should use such accounts to enchant ourselves with; and that is why I have already drawn out my tale so long."

At this point Socrates tells the disciples that all of them will sooner or later complete a similar journey. For him, this is the moment: he wants to bathe before drinking the poison, because he would prefer that the women not have the trouble of washing him after death. It's in this spirit that Socrates prepares himself and his disciples. When Crito asks how he would like to be buried, Socrates answers:

"Any way you like, that is, if you can catch me and I don't slip through your fingers!" and he laughs tranquilly and gently. Crito, he says, hasn't understood a word of his explanations. I am Socrates, the Socrates who is reasoning with you: he thinks that Socrates is the corpse he will soon see. But I will not be that body. I promised Athens that I would remain in prison and wouldn't flee, as Crito wanted me to do. But after my death, ah, then I will immediately go far from here, "blessed among the blessed." Bury me "as you please, in whatever way you think is most proper."

Followed by Crito, Socrates then moves into another room to have a bath, while the others await his return. After the bath, his children—two young and one older—are allowed to enter with the women, and he gives them instructions about carrying out his wishes, then he takes leave of them and rejoins his disciples. He speaks to them for a few minutes, and, just before sunset, the guard appears to announce that the time has come to drink the hemlock. The official is very embarrassed: he has learned to appreciate Socrates as "the noblest and gentlest" of all the prisoners who have come into his custody and says he's sure that Socrates won't be angry with him. Before going out he says goodbye and bursts into tears. Socrates says goodbye to him, in turn, and begs Crito to have the poison brought. Crito says no, the sun is still high on the mountains, and, besides, others have enjoyed dinner, wine, and company after receiving the announcement. But Socrates replies that there's no reason to delay, he wouldn't gain anything by drinking the hemlock a little later, and would be ridiculous in his own eyes if he became attached to life now and held on to it when there's nothing to hold on to. Crito obeys.

One of his slaves goes to summon the man who administers the poison. When he enters, Socrates asks him what he's supposed to do. He just has to drink, the man answers, and walk until he feels his legs getting heavy. At that point he'll lie down, and the poison will act by itself. Then he offers the cup to Socrates: who takes it cheerfully, without trembling, without changing color or expression, and asks if he can't make a libation to some god. There's no more liquid, the man says: we prepare only a sufficient dose. "I see," says Socrates. "But I suppose I am allowed, or rather bound, to pray the gods that my removal from this world to the other may be prosperous. This is my prayer, then; and I hope that it may be granted." While he utters these words Socrates empties the cup in one gulp, without showing any sign of disgust. Incapable of restraining themselves further, the disciples burst into tears, and he reproaches them jokingly: "Really, my friends, what a way to behave! Why, that was my main reason for sending away the women, to prevent this sort of discordant behavior; because I am told that one should make one's end in a reverent silence. Calm yourselves and be brave."

The disciples compose themselves. Socrates, his legs now heavy, lies down, the man who brought the poison pinches his feet and legs, keeping a hand on him. They can all see that Socrates' body is getting cold and stiffening. When the cold reaches his waist, Socrates uncovers his face and says to Crito: "We ought to offer a cock to Asclepius. See to it and don't forget." "No, it shall be done," Crito answers. "Are you sure that there is nothing else?" There is no response. The man uncovers him: his eyes are staring. Crito closes his mouth and eyes. "This," Phaedo tells Echecrates, "was the end of our comrade, who was, we may fairly say, of all those whom we knew in our time the bravest and also the wisest and the most just."

The trial and death of Socrates must have had enormous resonance in fifth-century Athens, as the version of the *Apology* composed by Xenophon attests. The absent disciple, Plato, however, orchestrates them with a flawless sense of drama, as if he were a Sophocles at work on *Oedipus the King* or, even more apt, *Oedipus at Colonus*. First comes the trial, with the passionate and reasoned— dialectic—defense of Socrates and the first echo of the theme of death. Then the *Crito*, where the law prevails over death. Finally, in the *Phaedo* Plato presents the long argument on the immortality of the soul and the death of Socrates in perfect counterpoint. The only thing that Xenophon's Socrates adds to this theme is that as Socrates leaves the judges he says to the weeping disciples: "Have you not known all along that from the moment of my birth nature had condemned me to death?" It's better to die now, Xenophon's Socrates maintains, than to live with the troubles of old age.

Plato's Socrates, as we've seen, is much more articulate. His first step is to say to the judges—we can imagine how they took it—that either death represents the end of everything or it opens the door to another world, which, as myth and traditional religion claim, must be happier than ours.

From the point of view of rational, philosophical discourse, there's no doubt that the three arguments used by Socrates—opposites, recollection, affinities—still constitute today the most satisfying rational response ever elaborated to this problem that torments us.

Still, it's clear that by the very end of the trial Socrates' inclination is gradually shifting away from total annihilation and toward the other world; once he has decided to remain in Athens and accept the death sentence, he moves toward life after death. The closer he gets to death, the more he talks about the immortality of the soul. And although this is increasingly the Socrates of Plato, as the allusions to Forms in the *Phaedo* indicate, the arguments in favor of the immortality of the soul are also of the type that the Socratic Socrates, so to speak, would have developed. These are rational arguments, based on pure logos, which *prove* beyond any reasonable doubt that the human soul is immortal.

Here Socrates enters the kingdom of *mýthos* (a word that he himself uses), of an argument, that is, that doesn't necessarily correspond to factual "truth" but is "very similar" to it. He seems willing to suspend disbelief. He claims, to all intents and purposes, that this "is worth the risk" and that "risk is noble" (*kalós*). A little earlier, he had said to his friends that to exorcise the fear of death they would have had to cast a "spell" on him every day to dissipate his fears. Now he proclaims that we should all enchant ourselves using the "mythical" accounts. We would associate risks and spells more closely with *Oedipus at Colonus* than with the Socrates of the Platonic dialogues, and yet here they are. Belief in the other world of tradition is worth the risk and the risk is noble. We should let ourselves be enchanted by the vision of this—as Dante would have called it—*status animarum post mortem*. It's a significant point, both in itself and because it anticipates the Christian imagination.

The story is not without pathos, and we could apply to it the observations of Longinus, who has a high regard for Plato's style and considers him "great," because he is "very Homeric." His intensity derives from the contrast between the feelings of Socrates' family and friends, on the one hand, and his own attitude, on the other. Women and disciples—and we with them—suffer and weep, while Socrates smiles, perfectly tranquil. The reader is struck by the simplicity and the serenity that emerge from the dramatic orchestration of the scenes and by the resonant power of the dialogue. The impression we get is that Socrates has digested death long before dying. The first in a long series of thinkers condemned to death by the authorities or by the people—Seneca, Hypatia, Boethius—Socrates has penetrated death, as if sliding into it, much more deeply than any other human being before him in Western culture.

It seems that thought needed the death of Socrates in order to fertilize itself and legitimately become philosophy. I don't have space here to illustrate these developments, but I would like to note briefly the most striking phases. Some decades after the *Phaedo*, Plato composes the *Timaeus*, one of his most beautiful dialogues and the only one that, thanks to the Latin translation of Calcidius, had the fortune to survive the catastrophe of the ancient world. The *Timaeus* is devoted to the "likely myth" of the origin and formation of the cosmos by the divinity, and has a fundamental importance for all the concepts of the Creation that are developed in the Middle Ages. It is suffused by a grand inspiration and punctuated by immensely compelling images. The passages I've chosen concern the structure of the universe, but the last shows what philosophy ultimately signifies. Here's the first:

Time came into being together with the Heaven, in order that, as they were brought into being together, so they may be dissolved together, if ever their dissolution should come to pass; and it is made after the pattern of the ever-enduring nature, in order that it may be as like that pattern as possible; for the pattern is a thing that has being for all eternity, whereas the Heaven has been and is and shall be perpetually throughout all time.

In virtue, then, of this plan and intent of the god for the birth of Time, in order that Time might be brought into being, Sun and Moon and five other stars—"wanderers," as they are called—were made to define and preserve the numbers of Time. Having made a body for each of them, the god set them in the circuits in which the revolution of the Different was moving—in seven circuits seven bodies. . .

For this reason came into being all the unwandering stars, living beings divine and everlasting, which abide for ever revolving uniformly upon themselves; while those stars that having turnings and in that sense "wander" came to be in the manner already described. . . . To describe the evolutions in the dance of these same gods, their juxtapositions, the counter-revolutions of their circles relatively to one another, and their advances; to tell which of the gods come into line with one another at their conjunctions, and which in opposition, and in what order they pass in front of or behind one another, and at what periods of time they are severally hidden from our sight and again reappearing send to men who cannot calculate panic fears and signs of things to come—to describe all this without visible models of these same would be labour spent in vain. So this much shall suffice on this head, and here let our account of the nature of the visible and generated gods come to an end.[30]

Plato the cosmologist is impressive: he possesses the capacity, extraordinary for a philosopher, to find the right image for an expansive, elaborate argument. Plato, says Longinus, knows how to expand: "extremely rich; like some ocean, he often swells into a mighty expanse of grandeur." He goes on: "I do not think there would have been so fine a bloom on Plato's philosophical doctrines, or that he would so often have embarked on poetic subject-matter and phraseology, had he not been striving heart and soul with Homer for first place, like a young contestant entering the ring with a long-admired champion." When, later, Plato identifies the beginning of philosophy, the exactness of observation expands in increasingly vast spirals:

The sight of day and night, of months and the revolving years, of equinox and solstice, has caused the invention of number and bestowed on us the notion of time and the study of the nature of the world; whence we have derived all philosophy, than which no greater boon has ever come or shall come to mortal man as a gift from heaven. This, then, I call the greatest benefit of eyesight; why harp upon all those things of less importance, for which one who loves not wisdom, if he were deprived of the sight of them, might "lament with idle moan"? For our part, rather let us speak of eyesight as the cause of this benefit for these ends: the god invented and gave us vision in order that we might observe the circuits of intelligence in the heaven and profit by them for the revolutions of our own thought, which are akin to them, though ours be troubled and they are unperturbed; and that, by learning to know them and acquiring the power to compute them rightly according to nature, we might reproduce the perfectly unerring revolutions of the god and reduce to settled order the wandering motions in ourselves.

Sight lets us contemplate the celestial movements, thus enabling the "circuits" of our mind to approach still closer to those of the Intelligence that superintends the heavens, and which they resemble, and allowing the birth of love of knowledge: of philosophy, the greatest good that humanity possesses. Finally, Plato associates voice and hearing with sight: they, too, Timaeus declares, "are a gift from heaven for the same intent and purpose. For not only was speech appointed to this same intent, to which it contributes in the largest measure, but also all that part of Music that is serviceable with respect to the hearing of sound is given for the sake of harmony." *Homo* would not be *sapiens* if he couldn't look at the stars. The resemblance between the "circuits of intelligence" and those of the human mind denotes the "love of knowledge," philosophy: and this is the greatest celebration of philosophical inquiry.

The third thinker of the Greek crown is Aristotle, the disciple of Plato, as Plato had been of Socrates. Plato thinks that a hyperuranian reality exists (that is, the world of ideas, and the world we live in is only its shadow), while Aristotle believes that the true reality is the one we live in: the objects we see and touch are "what is," individual and universal at the same time. Plato is convinced that in the final analysis poetry is a deception. Aristotle considers it more serious and philosophical than history because it speaks of the universal. But Plato and Aristotle are in perfect agreement about the purposes, ends, and happiness that philosophy entails, and these passages are the evidence that Greek thought, which grew up with Socrates and reached maturity with Plato and then Aristotle, celebrates itself—celebrates thinking, celebrates philosophy—in a manner unsurpassed before and perhaps after, because philosophy is a true, and remarkable, discovery.

Aristotle, a writer averse to Platonic flights, sometimes manages to concentrate in a single sentence the full essence of a long meditation. For example, in the *Metaphysics*, summarizing the path that man must travel to reach the good: "We ought to act in such a way that, starting with the individual good, the general good becomes the individual good." When we stop to consider this statement, we realize that it is the summation of an entire ethics. If this rule were to be respected, human behavior would reach ethical heights never before attained.

Yet Aristotle can also expound broadly. In the *Nicomachean Ethics* he declares that the primary goal of man is happiness. But how do we get there? And what does the greatest happiness consist in? Well, I will give a brief overview for those in a hurry, leaving others to enjoy the text. If happiness is an activity in accordance with virtue, it's reasonable, Aristotle writes, that it should be in accordance with the highest virtue. And this will be the virtue of our better part, the intellect, which guides us and possesses something of the divine. Thus the activity of the intellect, in accordance with the virtue that is proper to it, must be perfect happiness. In other words, perfect happiness is a contemplative activity: not action, not governing, not administering justice, and not even, naturally, drinking, eating, or making love, but contemplation. The perfect happiness of man, according to Aristotle, lies in contemplation, here, on the earth, now:

If happiness is an activity in accordance with virtue, it is reasonable to assume that it is in accordance with the highest virtue, and this will be the virtue of the best part of us. Whether this is the intellect or something else that we regard as naturally ruling and guiding us, and possessing insight into things noble and divine—either as being actually divine itself or as being more divine than any other part of us—it is the activity of this part, in accordance with the virtue proper to it, that will be perfect happiness.

We have already said that it is a contemplative activity. This may be regarded as consonant both with our earlier arguments and with the truth. For contemplation is both the highest form of activity (since the intellect is the highest thing in us, and the objects that it apprehends are the highest things that can be known), and also it is the most continuous, because we are more capable of continuous contemplation than we are of any practical activity. Also we assume that happiness must contain an admixture of pleasure; now activity in accordance with <philosophic> wisdom is admittedly the most pleasant of the virtuous activities; at any rate philosophy is held to entail pleasures that are marvelous in purity and permanence; and it stands to reason that those who possess knowledge pass their time more pleasantly than those who are still in pursuit of it. Again, the quality that we call self-sufficiency will belong in the highest degree to the contemplative activity. The wise man, no less than the just one and all the rest, requires the necessaries of life; but, given an adequate supply of these, the just man also needs people with and towards whom he can perform just actions, and similarly with the temperate man, the brave man and each of the others; but the wise man can practice contemplation by himself, and the wiser he is, the more he can do it. No doubt he does it better with the help of fellow-workers; but for all that he is the most self-sufficient of men. Again, contemplation would seem to be the only activity that is appreciated for its own sake; because nothing is gained from it except the act of contemplation, whereas from practical activities we expect to gain something more or less over and above the action.

Also it is commonly believed that happiness depends on leisure;

because we occupy ourselves so that we may have leisure, just as we make war in order that we may live at peace. Now the exercise of the practical virtues takes place in politics or in warfare, and these professions seem to have no place for leisure. This is certainly true of the military profession, for nobody chooses to make war or provokes it for the sake of making war; a man would be regarded as a bloodthirsty monster if he made his friends into enemies in order to bring about battles and slaughter. The politician's profession also makes leisure impossible, since besides the business of politics it aims at securing positions of power and honour, or the happiness of the politician himself and of his fellow-citizens—a happiness separate from politics, and one which we clearly pursue as separate.

If, then, politics and warfare, although pre-eminent in nobility and grandeur among practical activities in accordance with goodness, are incompatible with leisure and, not being desirable in themselves, are directed towards some other end, whereas the activity of the intellect is considered to excel in seriousness, taking as it does the form of contemplation, and to aim at no other end beyond itself and to possess a pleasure peculiar to itself, which intensifies its activity; and if it is evident that self-sufficiency and leisuredness and such freedom from fatigue as is humanly possible, together with all other attributes assigned to the supremely happy man, are those that accord with this activity; then this activity will be the perfect happiness for man—provided that it is allowed a full span of life; for nothing that pertains to happiness is incomplete.

But such a life will be too high for human attainment; for any man who lives it will do so not as a human being but in virtue of something divine within him, and in proportion as this divine element is superior to the composite being, so will its activity be superior to that of the other kind of virtue. So if the intellect is divine compared with man, the life of the intellect must be divine compared with the life of a human being. And we ought not to listen to those who warn us that "man should think the thoughts of man," or "mortal thoughts fit mortal minds"; but we ought, so far as in us lies, to put on immortality, and do all that we can to live in conformity with the highest that is in us; for even if it is small in bulk, in power and preciousness it far excels all the rest. Indeed it would seem that this is the true self of the individual, since it is the authoritative and better part of him; so it would be an odd thing if a man chose to live someone else's life instead of his own. Moreover, what we said above will apply here too: that what is best and most pleasant for any given creature is that which is proper to it. Therefore for man, too, the best and most pleasant life is the life of the intellect, since the intellect is in the fullest sense the man. So this life will also be the happiest.[31]

It's no coincidence that this thinker will be called "the master of those who know." He opens the great project of the *Metaphysics* with the memorable sentence "By nature all men long to know." He unites philosophy, science, and poetry in the principle that moves them: wonder. And, in a letter written in old age, Aristotle declares that, the older and more solitary he is, the more he becomes a "lover of myth."

VIII
WE, I, THEY, HE: THE LYRIC

He looks to me to be in heaven,
That man who sits across from you
And listens near you to your soft speaking,

Your laughing lovely: that, I vow,
Makes the heart leap in my breast;
For watching you a moment, speech fails me,

My tongue is paralysed, at once
A light fire runs beneath my skin,
My eyes are blinded, and my ears drumming,

The sweat pours down me, and I shake
All over, sallower than grass:
I feel as if I'm not far off dying.

But no thing is too hard to bear . . . [32]

We'll begin our discussion of the *I*'s entrance into
poetry with one of the longest fragments of Sappho's lyric
poems. The *Iliad* and the *Odyssey*, as we've seen, are third-
person narratives, in which a poet or bard recounts the
adventures of the protagonists. Lyric poetry, instead, tends
to be in the first person, singular or plural, *I* or *we*,

monodic or choral: a composition accompanied by string instruments (lyre, zither, or harp), a song for several voices or for one. Sappho's poetry is monadic, and intensely ego-centric. She describes her own feelings and her own reactions. She sees a man talking with his beloved and is gripped by tremendous emotion: a leap of the heart, fire under the skin, tongue paralyzed, sweat pouring down, a drumming in her ears, blindness, shaking. Whether or not it's a wedding song, the lovesickness of the person, the poet, who says "I" inhabits the poem. All Sappho's poetry is like that, but it may also be useful to see what the author of *On the Sublime* wrote about this lyric:

Are you not astonished at the way in which, as though they were gone from her and belonged to another, she at one and the same time calls up soul and body, ears, tongue, eyes, and skin; how, uniting opposites, she freezes while she burns, is both out of her senses and in her right mind? And all this is done so that not one emotion alone may be seen in her, but a concourse of emotions. All such emotions are experienced by lovers, but it is, as I said, the selection of the most striking of them and their fusion into a single whole that have given the poem its distinction.

As Longinus understood, Sappho brilliantly creates *all-absorbing* poetry. Not all the Greek lyric poets had the power to do this, but all of them, in different ways, discovered, and highlighted, what Bruno Snell called "individuality." They dug deeply into both their own minds and the external world; this was true, evidently, in all the lyric genres. Elegies and iambs shouldn't, strictly speaking, be called lyrics, but from the start Archilocus, the virtuoso composer of elegies and iambs, was part of later canons, and so all the others are considered an integral part of the Greek lyric canon. That canon includes some of the masters of the lyric, from the Alexandrian era on, as the *Greek Anthology* celebrates them:

Pindar, holy mouth of the Muses, and thou, Bacchylides, garrulous Siren, and ye, Aeolian graces of Sappho; pen of Anacreon, and thou, Stesichorus, who in thy works didst draw off Homer's stream; honeyed page of Simonides, and thou, Ibycus, who didst cull the sweet bloom of Persuasion and of the love of lads; sword of Alcaeus, that didst often shed the blood of tyrants, defending his country's laws, and ye nightingales of Alcman, singing ever of maidens; look kindly on me, ye authors and finishers of all lyric song.[33]

The name of the elegiac poet Mimnermus isn't here, but Mimnermus, too, sings of love with great power, and the opening of his "What's life" is memorable. This lyric is a kind of counterpart of Sappho's: an exaltation of the male eros where, in spite of the second line, the "I" is really a "we." The "secret closeness, tender favours, bed" are the "flowers that grace youth's prime" not for Mimnermus alone but for all of us, and in all of us they are followed by "painful" old age:

What's life, what's joy, without love's heavenly gold?
I hope I die when I no longer care
For secret closeness, tender favours, bed,
Which are the rapturous flowers that grace youth's prime
For men and women. But when painful age
Comes on, that makes a man loathsome and vile,
malignant troubles ever vex his heart;

seeing the sunlight gives him joy no more.
He is abhorred by boys, by women scorned:
So hard a thing God made old age to be.

With reason, Mimnermus is the poet of life's transience, and he draws on the famous simile between leaves and human generations in the *Iliad*, but takes a step forward with respect to Homer:

But we are like the leaves that flowery spring
Puts forth, quick spreading in the sun's warm light:
For a brief span of time we take our joy
in our youth's bloom, the future, good or ill,
kept from us, while the twin dark Dooms stand by,
one bringing to fulfillment harsh old age,
the other death. The ripeness of youth's fruit
is short, short as the sunlight on the earth,
and once this season of perfection's past,
it's better to be dead than stay alive.
All kinds of worry come. One man's estate
is failing, and there's painful poverty;
another has no sons—the keenest need
one feels as one goes down below the earth;
sickness wears down another's heart. There's none
Zeus does not give a multitude of ills.

This is not only a personal lyric. The poet doesn't say "I," he says "we": the entire human race. The image comes from Book VI of the *Iliad*, where, as we've seen, Glaucus uses it in answer to Diomedes, who, before the duel starts, asks him his lineage. "Why do you ask my lineage?" Glaucus replies:

"Like the generations of leaves, the lives of mortal men.
Now the wind scatters the old leaves across the earth,
now the living timber bursts with the new buds
and spring comes round again. And so with men:
as one generation comes to life, another dies away."

Glaucus is speaking of the human generations. Not Mimnermus. Mimnermus speaks of *the life of each one of us*: it's our life that resembles the leaves: there is the flower, there is the moment when the leaves are beautiful, green, luxuriant, then youth passes and old age arrives. Now the leaf withers, turns yellow, is about to die. It's the single individual who resembles the leaves: who, like them, changes and declines, withers, enduring the ills of old age. Mimnermus composes a beautiful lyric on the brevity of life. He employs the same image of man that the sapiential books of the Bible developed. "Man that is born of woman," says Job, "is of few days, and full of trouble. He comes forth like a flower, and withers; he flees like a shadow, and continues not." This trope of the leaves, descending from Mimnermus to Virgil and beyond, also picks up a biblical inheritance and is then given new life with Dante and Shakespeare, among others. "That time of year thou mayst in me behold," Shakespeare writes, "when yellow leaves, or none, or few, do hang / upon those boughs which shake against the cold."

Reading Mimnermus now, in the twenty-first century, we may have the impression of listening to Bob Dylan, or Leonard Cohen. The themes of his elegies are the same as those of Dylan and Cohen. The tone, with an undercurrent of ironic melancholy, is often similar. Mimnermus celebrates youth and abhors old age, like the man of today. His lyric speaks of the I, but also often of the we. When the "we" refers to poets, singers, dancing girls, or those immersed in the natural world, the lyric becomes choral, and in place of Mimnermus we would have Alcman, one of the greatest lyric poets of all time.

In a very famous fragment Alcman declares that, now that he's old, he'd like to be a kingfisher, the male of the halcyon, which, according to ancient legend, is transported over the sea by the female of the species:

My legs can support me no longer, young ladies
with voices of honey and song divine!
Ah, would that I could be a kingfisher, flying
sea-blue, fearless, amid you halcyons
down to rest on the foaming brine!

Alcman confesses to those same girls, who in the past he had inspired to dance, that he will no longer do so, and he compares himself to the kingfisher who, when old, will rely on the female and fly with her help. Alcman was used to leading the dance, singing the song he had composed for the occasion. Unable to participate, he is forced to give up the performative aspect of his poetry, at the ritual, sacred moment when it becomes public movement and voice, while the poem's resonance is reduced in his eyes to a minimum.

This flight means that the fragility of old age is transported back to a youth now past but rendered accessible again thanks to the young women of the chorus; it means becoming a strong and resolute man again. And it means possessing again the "sea-blue" color of the water's depths, caressing its surface, absorbing its reflection. It means, finally, thanks to the female halcyon, being newly present to poetry, possessing its light once more: composing with a swift and delicate touch, like grazing the water.

The first line of the fragment is shadowed by sadness. Then, once the poet's desire has been expressed, a quiet joy manifests itself—the enraptured exultation in the vicarious flight—and reaches the apex in two key expressions, *haliporphyros,* "sea-blue," and *epi kymatos anthos*, literally, "above the flower of the waves." The first, a word already used, with reference to fabrics, in Books VI and XIII of the *Odyssey*, could be better translated as "the luminosity of the sea," or "blinding dazzle of the sea." But if that word catches us unaware, referring to a bird that has been transformed into one of the sea's reflections, the other is the true surprise, the "flower of the waves," which strikes us dumb with wonder. Only a Greek could imagine that the wave, rising up in foam, was crowned by a flower and, rolling over, revealed the corolla of a flower.

The library in Alexandria—all the libraries of the ancient world—must have possessed papyrus scrolls containing the lyric poems produced by the archaic poets: we have only fragments quoted by others: encyclopedists, grammarians, collectors of curiosities. Yet even from the few remaining passages we can get an idea of the extraordinary force this poetry has, and understand how later poets, first in the Greek world, then in the Roman, tried to imitate it. The Latins, finally, were able to collect the ancient inheritance and transmit it to the Middle Ages and hence to modernity. We are third- or fourth-degree heirs, but are still amazed by the archaic poetic words.

Let's read, then, a final fragment of Alcman, the so-called "Nocturne":

They sleep, the mountain peaks,
the clefts, ridges, and gullies,
and all the creatures that the dark earth feeds,
the animals of the glen, the tribe of bees,
the monsters of the salt purple deeps.
They sleep, the tribes of winging birds.

Alcman doesn't even try to depict a night where the light of the moon and stars illuminates vast expanses. Instead, he concentrates on the quiet of the world. He obtains a surprising effect by repeating "they sleep" in the last line. Then he attributes to sleep what is not subject to it: mountain peaks, clefts, ridges, gullies, glen. When he introduces the animals, he situates them on the "dark earth." Then, suddenly, he widens the space, obliquely indicating, after the earth, the sea and the air. He names wild beasts, bees, fish, birds: that is, the entire animal world.

For us this is only a marvelous fragment; we don't know how it continued or where its place was in the poem. In the context of the archaic lyric poem, it's unlikely that the description was an end in itself; it's probable, rather, that a human being's restlessness was contrasted with it, following what will soon become a commonplace: quiet governs all living beings, but the heroine, or hero, is tormented. Or, with the introduction of the first person singular: all the world sleeps, I alone am restless, awake.

At this stage, there is neither "I" nor "we." There is, instead, the sleep of the world, overpowering. Here, we should return to Sappho and compare her nocturnes to Alcman's works to get an idea of the development of the Greek lyric poem. But first we may recall that, from the start, the lyric was also concerned with themes very different from love and the transience of human life. Among the elegiac poets, for example, are Solon, Theognis, and Xenophanes: the first the poet of justice and political action; the second of physical Eros, on the one hand, and, on the other, of friendship as a political-social alliance among aristocrats; the third, who is also a pre-Socratic thinker, a celebrant of the gods, of All, of nature. "The gods have not revealed all things to men from the beginning," Xenophanes says, "but by seeking they find in time what is better"; "One god, the greatest among gods and men, neither in form like unto mortals nor in thought."

We find still greater variety if we consider poets like Tyrtaeus, Ibycus, Anacreon, Archilocus, and Alcaeus. It's not merely a matter of variety: incisiveness is what counts; and nearly every line results in the exploration of a new aspect. Tyrtaeus is famous principally because he proclaimed, "For it is fine to die in the front line, a brave man fighting for his fatherland," but to this he adds the importance of defending one's family. Ibycus recounts the doings of Polycrates, the tyrant of Samos, but he can also introduce extraordinary images, like those of spring and the old horse:

In spring the Cydonian quince trees
watered from freshets of rivers
where Nymphs have their virginal gardens
blossom, and vine shoots are growing
under the shade of the branches.
But Love in me at no season is laid to rest.

Like the North Wind of Thrace that comes blazing
with lightning, he rushes upon me,
sent by the Cyprian goddess
with withering frenzies, dark-lowering,
undaunted, and from the foundations
he overwhelms and devastates my heart.

Once again Love, as he looks at me meltingly
under dark eyelashes, tries to induce me
with every enticement to enter the Cyprian goddess's endless hunting net.
By heaven, I tremble upon his approach
like a champion horse who is feeling his age
and is led once again to the chariot yoke for a race.

In both images Ibycus praises the irresistible force of
Eros, not as simply falling in love but as a cosmic power
that overwhelms everything, with the "withering frenzies"
and "every enticement" of Aphrodite. But the lines contain
an overabundance, an expressive *excess* that mirrors that
overwhelming in irresistible crescendo: the quince trees
grow "watered from freshets of rivers"; the flowers of the
vine "are growing under the shade of the branches." Every
object is accompanied by a detail that concretely *demon-
strates* its bursting growth up to the moment when Eros is
freed even of spring and explodes, blazing with lightning
like the North Wind. Which still blows—so it seems to us,

reading—on the poet as he approaches old age: a horse accustomed to winning races, now old, trembling, yoked, and shaken by Eros.

With Anacreon the variations on the erotic theme become virtuosic. We need only compare the vision of a girl on Lesbos and that of the beloved boy:

Once again the gold-haired Eros
targets me with his crimson playball
and invites me to sport with a certain
braided-sandalled girl.

But she, being from the noble island
of Lesbos, only turns her nose up
at my white hair; she is gawping
after some other lass . . .

O lad with the look of a lass,
I seek you, but you don't heed,
Not knowing you hold the reins
of my soul, my life.

Almost mirrorlike, the fragments seem like "jokes" at first. They aren't at all, though, if we consider Anacreon's prayer to Dionysus to make Cleobulus accept his love: with Dionysus you don't joke.

The legendary lightness of so much Greek lyric poetry doesn't construct jokes: rather, it plays with seriousness, to prevent it from becoming "serious." When Alcaeus praises the Hebrus, "loveliest of all rivers," because it's frequented by girls who "scoop" you, "water divine that kisses them like balm," while "with tender hands" they "sluice their pretty thighs," the flash of light is dazzling: here it's not excess, as in Ibycus, but subtraction, the vision a peek, synecdoche. Alcaeus also knows how to present a complete view: a hall of weapons, a shipwreck, a winter storm. And he is capable of the rapid stroke: "Now we must drink with might and main, get drunk, for Myrsilus is dead"; "pure Sappho with violet hair, who sweetly smiles."

Alcaeus refers inevitably to his predecessor Archilochus, with whom he has in common various themes and, naturally, the famous image of the shield left unwillingly "by a bush." Archilochus has a latitude such that one cannot hope to contain it in a few lines. He is the poet whom the author of *On the Sublime* compares even to Homer for his description of a shipwreck. Archilochus' virtuosity shines everywhere: he was the first and best composer of iambs, and perhaps the greatest of the Greek lyric poets. Evidence of this is a passage describing the eclipse of the sun (of 648 B.C.), which immediately becomes a comment on how human beings can be gripped by terror and how from then on anything might be believable. This "anything" unfolds in three lines that present three pairs of impossibilities:

There's nothing now you can't expect, nothing's against the odds,
there are no miracles, now Zeus the father of the gods
has turned the noonday into night and hidden the bright sun
out of the sky, so clammy dread came over everyone.
From now on all is credible, and like enough to be:
Let none of you now be surprised at anything you see,
not even if land animals switch to where dolphins roam,

and the salt sea and the crashing waves become their chosen home, while dolphins take a fancy to the mountains and the trees.

An eclipse of the sun goes against all the ordinary rules of the natural world, and so from now on man can expect any phenomenon: in particular an exchange of habitat. Archilochus' tour de force, it should be noted, doesn't have a fundamentally scientific motivation—it's not an attempt to explain to readers how an eclipse works. This is relevant, because the century between the seventh and sixth B.C. was crucial in the development of the pre-Socratic thinkers' investigation of nature. On the other hand, the passage doesn't have an explicit personal poetic intention, either, in the sense that it doesn't point to a correspondence or a divergence between the cosmos and the I. It seems to be, instead, the clever exploitation of a popular cliché: there is an eclipse of the sun, nothing is predictable anymore, nothing can surprise us.

So at last, inevitably, we return for a moment to Sappho's poetry. Sappho is so elegant, precise, and evocative in her treatment of the I and its position in the universe that she seems to be present at the birth of a new world.

The stars about the lovely moon
Withdraw and hide their shining forms,
When at her full she bathes the earth in light.[34]

The moon has set, and the Pleiades;
it is midnight,
time is passing,
and I sleep alone.[35]

Here is Sappho, alone in the night. There is almost no ancient poet who can equal Sappho when it comes to nocturnal poetry, with the exception, naturally, of Homer. We can't help being reminded of the celebrated simile at the end of Book VIII of the *Iliad*, in which the Trojans, having advanced on the Greek camp, stop for the night, before unleashing the perhaps decisive attack, and light watchfires, which appear as numerous and bright as the stars in the sky, while the light of the moon delineates all the features of the landscape. (I discussed this in the first chapter.)

Sappho, who knows the Homeric passage very well, doesn't do that. She shows us a night experienced by the "I": the moon and the Pleiades have set, the night is midway in its course: and *Sappho sleeps alone*. The basic point is not only the stars and the moon: it's the fact that she is sleeping in solitude, bitterly, without a companion. Yet Sappho is brilliant—as almost no one has been since—in the absolutely essential description of the night. The construction of these four- or five-line fragments is so astonishing that if they hadn't originally been part of longer poems—as they certainly were—they could be considered almost Japanese haiku.

In the first of the two fragments I've just cited, Sappho contradicts, or corrects, Homer, noting that the stars hide their luminous faces when the moon shines brighter. During a full moon—the observation is banal—the stars, especially those closer to the moon, are less visible. Homer didn't make a distinction: for him stars and moon were part of a single light. Sappho, instead, does make a distinction—she really does! Precise and accurate, she remains intimate and elegant. Homer sheds nocturnal light profusely, with divine abundance, on an entire world; Sappho contains the world as if it were in her own eyes and her own hands. Homer invents a shepherd who, observing the night scene—we don't know from where or how—rejoices. Ideally, Sappho takes the place of that shepherd.

But Sappho sleeps alone. That's what brings the "I" to the fore: that's what we'll never forget. With Sappho asleep in the middle of the night, after the moon and the Pleiades have set, the modern lyric begins: which, through Latin and medieval times, the Provençal poets and Petrarch, will occupy European poetry up to Romanticism.

The *I* is onstage at last; it was in the background before. But Greek lyric poetry, naturally, doesn't speak only of the *I*. It also concerns the *we*. Simonides of Ceos, perhaps the first professional poet, is famous for his epigrams, in which the transience of human life is powerfully stressed:

Man's strength is but little, and futile his concerns,
his lifespan short, filled with trouble on trouble;
and over it death, inescapable, uniform, looms,
to be dispensed in equal shares
to high and low alike.

As you are mortal, don't ever affirm what tomorrow will bring,
or how long the man that you see in good fortune will keep it:
not even the wing-spreading housefly
changes perch so fast.

And yet Simonides is also the author of the ode for the dead of Thermopylae, the three hundred Spartans who in

480 B.C., under the command of Leonidas, sacrificed themselves to slow the invasion of Greece by the Persians and their leader, Xerxes. It's a famous passage, and has been carved into a stone right beside the road that crosses the pass:

τῶν ἐν Θερμοπύλαις θανόντων
εὐκλεὴς μὲν ἁ τύχα, καλὸς δ᾽ὁ πότμος

Of those who died at Thermopylae
fame is their fortune, fair their fate,
their tomb an altar; in the place of wailing
there is remembrance, and their dirge is praise.
This winding sheet is such
as neither mold nor Time that conquers all
can fade; this sepulchre
of fine men has adopted as its sacristan
Greece's good name. Witness Leonidas,
the king of Sparta: he has left
a monument of valor, and perennial fame.

There is nothing, perhaps, more classical and noble than this epitaph, with the repetitive structure of the second, third, and fourth lines, in which every noun with a potentially negative meaning ("fortune" and "fate") is paired with a word that reverses the connotation ("fame" and "fair"), while the words of sacrifice and sorrow ("tomb," "wailing," "dirge") are transformed into altar, remembrance, praise: in the poem of Simonides himself and of all Greece. That thematic structure of the poem's central lines is repeated with variations: the action of time *pandamátor* ("that conquers all") and of "mold," which incarnates it on human monuments, is negated by virtue of poetry, the "winding sheet" that allows us to go beyond the horizons of man—and here are the "witnesses," Leonidas and his men, who now live in the "sepulchre," "Greece's good name." They are "*fine* men," the text proclaims literally, who at Thermopylae delivered the beauty (the "monument") of *areté* and *kléos*, valor ("virtue") and glory.

Simonides makes poetry of *them*: in Athens at the decisive moments of the war against the Persians, he praises the Spartans. But this "them" has become *us*: "Greece's good name." Bacchylides (who is the nephew of Simonides) and Pindar create, instead, poetry of the *him*, the winner of a contest at the Games that are held regularly, in conjunction with festivals, in various localities in Greece: Olympia, Delphi (Pythian), Corinth (Isthmian), Nemea. It's as if a modern poet or bard were to celebrate an athlete who won the long jump at the Olympics, or a cyclist, a soccer player, a race-car driver. The difference lies in the fact that the modern author sings the praises of an athlete of the past who has become a "myth." The ancient poet, instead, celebrates—for a fee—an event of the present: which, by virtue of that celebration, attains the stature of myth.

The author of *On the Sublime* asked: "In lyric poetry would you choose to be Bacchylides rather than Pindar?" Of course not, Western tradition answered, burying the first under a blanket of oblivion and exalting the second. Reading Pindar twenty-five hundred years after he composed his odes is a unique experience. Take, for example, the *First Pythian*, composed for the victory of Hieron of Syracuse in the chariot race at Delphi, in 470 B.C. The ode opens with the famous exaltation of the golden lyre and the music that possesses the singer and is possessed by Apollo and the Muses: an enveloping glow spreads from here over the entire poem and immediately, in the first stanza, reverberates like a flash in its own brightness, stifling even the "warlike thunderbolt of ever-flowing fire," the greatest privilege of the highest God. The lyre, which the bards, the poets, can only obey, starts the dance, and with its music puts to sleep (in the first antistrophe) the eagle on Zeus's scepter; soothes Ares, the god of war; and charms all the gods.

We're stunned by this opening: and we'd like to stop and listen again to the song of the *chrýsea phórminx*; look for a moment longer at the Muses, who with their violet hair serve as background to the gilded aura of the lyre; understand how the lyre can extinguish God's lightning and its eternal flame, put an eagle to sleep, and calm every fight, every clash, every war. But Pindar gives no way out, pressing with the vision of music and poetry from the opposite direction: all the "creatures unloved by Zeus shudder when they hear the Pierians' voice, whether on earth or in the relentless sea," he warns in the first epode. The Muses are terrifying for those who don't have divine favor, especially for Typhos, the monster with a hundred heads, who first lived in a cave in Asia Minor and now lies in Tartarus, crushed between the Campanian coasts of Cumae and Sicily, where "the pillar of snow-covered Etna, rearing to heaven . . . pins him down": Etna, the volcano that looms over the whole island and Italy's western sea.

Here we are, suddenly transported from the glow of the lyre and the peaks of Olympus to the cavities of the planet, to the immense mass of the mountain that presses on land

and water, and on which the air, in turn, weighs: to Etna, "yearlong nurse of freezing snow" and inexhaustible source of fire (thus the thought flashes through our mind that the four elements are bound together in a *point* that is also an entire *world*). The second strophe and the first part of the antistrophe are devoted to the eruption of the volcano: maybe the one a few years earlier, which Pindar could have witnessed in person, and which leaves a powerful imprint also on the *Prometheus* of Aeschylus. In this passage fire becomes incandescent liquid: a river of lava and smoke by day, a red current that at night descends to the sea. The words roll here like boulders swept along by the flames, and poetry becomes magma that, flowing, "spouts forth terrifying torrents of Hephaestus' fire" in the air: the spectacle is not only a "prodigious portent" for those who have seen it but also a "wonder" for those who hear of it, who "listen" to tales about it from the witnesses. The lyre's spellbinding melody is now replaced, even in the sounds of the words, by a horrendous "din," while its gold has literally become, as the *First Olympian* says, "like blazing fire in the night." That flame flashes now from underground: it's not the fire of the divine glow, which we recall extinguished by the lyre. No longer "eternal," it has become matter, but a kind of primal matter, suspended amid the four elements, amid liquid, solid, and gaseous states, and so always inaccessible, and with "sacred" sources "that cannot be approached":

From its depths spew sacred founts of fire that cannot be approached; by day rivers pour forth lurid streaks of smoke,

and by night a crimson rolling flame sweeps down rocks,
which crash into the sea's broad expanse.
That monster spouts forth terrifying torrents of Hephaestus' fire—
a prodigious portent to behold, and a wonder for visitors to hear.
Such a thing is imprisoned between Aetna's dark-wooded peaks and
    its plain,
and the bed he lies on gouges and galls the whole length of his back.[36]

Matter that is *here* and *now*: and which from the remote
recesses of the myth—in which Zeus punishes Typhos, who
has threatened the order of the cosmos, by hurling him into
Tartarus—penetrates Sicily's geological past and present
(the bed still "gouges and galls" the back of the beast
today), and from snow-capped Etna with its leafy slopes
flows down to the plain and the sea—to the city of Etna
founded by Hieron.

Pindar has compelled us to continuous parentheses, to
interpolations that interrupt his flow, to follow him, trying
to maintain parallel and intersecting gazes that are open,
functioning, and moving. Along with the Aeschylus of
Prometheus, he in effect invented the eruption of Etna for
all of Western literature, and readers coming to his poems
for the first time have just had a burning, unforgettable
experience. Longinus says that Pindar and Sophocles, in
their creative transport, inflame everything. Well, the
expression should be understood, in this case, in a literal
sense: Pindar has created a flaming magma of words. Ovid,
Virgil, Seneca, and the author of the *Sublime* himself
attempted to imitate him in vain.

Pindar, meanwhile, hasn't stopped: with a shorter leap,

he finally lands, temporarily, on the Pythian Games, where the ruler of Syracuse has won, and is proclaimed by the herald, in Delphi, "founder" of the city of Etna. Right in the middle of the second antistrophe, however, between Typhos who lies under the volcano, and Hieron, who rises victorious in the Pythian contest and erects his city at the foot of the mountain, is Zeus, who reigns sovereign "over this mountain" and to whom the poet prays for himself (as if he were frightened, says the scholiast, by the story of the monster's end) and for the king of Syracuse: Zeus, who subdued Typhos and dominated the beginning of the poem with the lightning bolt and the eagle.

We seem to have come in sight of the event, the chariot race, and the victory and the glory we've been waiting for from the start. Yet we've barely departed, on the one hand, and, on the other, have arrived far beyond, in the future. "For men who sail in ships," Pindar writes in the second epode, "the first sign of favor as they embark is the rising of a following wind, because then there is a fair chance that they will enjoy a safe return." It's odd but psychologically true that those who are departing think of their return just at the moment of departure: and so for him a favorable wind is *cháris*, grace and joy. The poet, who from the beginning has been thinking of the end, aiming at a "safe return"—at a journey completed, a perfect circle—always gazes, like the eagle, into the distance, into the future: in *these* matters, that is, the current circumstances of Hieron's victory, his words bring hope that the city of Etna will be famous in the future for "crowns won with horses, and renowned for its festivals of sweet music." Apollo is called on to preside over that future, and over the present of the song that opens and prefigures it. He has already been invoked, at one with the lyre and the Muses, in the first line of the ode: lord of Lycia, Delos, and Delphi (and so of the entire Hellenic world), god of light and shadow, sovereign of "Castalia's spring at Parnassus," of prophecy, of music, and of poetry: "be willing to store *my wish* in your heart and make *this a land* of brave men."

At this point we might expect (we're now at the start of the third strophe) to return to the charm of the opening, to the lyre that is the instrument of Phoebus. But that happens only obliquely, and for a single instant. The third strophe, tied to the invocations to Zeus and Apollo in the preceding antistrophe and epode, opens in fact with a maxim, a *gnóme*, at once metaphysical and ethical, stating that all human "virtues"—wisdom, skill in competition and war, art of the word—depend on the divine: "All mortal achievement stems from the gods' designs: thus are born skilled poets and men of strong hands and great eloquence." Only now does Pindar return to poetry, to the song of praise uttered by the golden lyre, and he uses for it the image of the javelin throw. The true poet has to know the just measure, and not hurl his lines too far. He must beat his rivals, like a runner, and win the contest, certainly, but not go "outside the field":

Eager to praise that famous man, I hope I do not, as one might say,
throw the bronze-tipped javelin I spin with my hand outside the field
     of play,
but surpass my competitors by the length of my cast.

In the same way, Pindar hopes that "all future time" will give Hieron prosperity and an abundance of riches (but it is the gods invoked at the beginning of the strophe who will bestow it), and above all "forgetfulness of past hardship." Finally, in the third antistrophe, the poet concentrates on Hieron, praising him, and recalling his "unflinching spirit" in combat, when, with his brother Gelon and "the gods' help," they won fame and crowned it with wealth (the two ideals of aristocracy), more than any other Greeks: decisively defeating (it's barely an allusion in the text) the Carthaginians, led by Hamilcar, at Himera in 480, and the Etruscans at Cumae, referred to later, for control of the Italian seas.

Thus from the enchantment of the lyre, from the myth of Typhos and the eruption of Etna, from the Delphic Games, we have arrived at *history*, the moment when Syracuse became the superpower of the Greek West. Pindar immediately offers an equivalent in *myth*, flying back in time to Philoctetes, the hero crucial in the defeat of Troy who was abandoned by the Greeks, completely alone, on the island of Lemnos, because of the smell that came from his wound: Hieron, ill and perhaps limping, like the mythic archer, "went to war like Philoctetes," carried by "godlike heroes."

A moment later, the Muse is invoked for the fourth time in the ode: may the poet, traveling in her chariot, raise a "song" also to Deinomenes, Hieron's son, whom he installed as ruler of the new city of Etna (Pindar calls him "king"), because "his father's victory is no alien joy." Gelon, Hieron, and Deinomenes now emerge, on the poetic-historical horizon, as a real Syracusan dynasty, fundamental for Greece and the Mediterranean.

Hieron founded Etna for Deinomenes, Pindar continues in the fourth strophe, "with god-built freedom," and "according to the ordinances of Hyllus," the son of Heracles, and of Aegimius, that is, of the two founders of the line of Dorians who colonized the ancient Peloponnese and, in particular, Sparta. Again with unparalleled rapidity, Pindar sketches in a few lines the Doric conquest of Greece, from Mt. Pindus in the north to Amyclae, near Sparta, in the south: there, under the heights of Taygetus, their descendants—the acclaimed neighbors of the Dioscuri Castor and Pollux, "of the white horses"—will obey the ancestral laws; and there "the fame of their spears" increased. After Philoctetes and the mythical heroes of the Trojan War, Pindar again takes up the genealogical roots and the ethnic story of the Achaeans. Tied to it are the rules that tradition, custom, and law have established for the Dorians, and which find their institutional model in aristocratic Sparta: Pindar sees that "constitutional wisdom" applied, on foundations of freedom constructed by the gods and therefore inalienable, in Etna, too, which Hieron has populated with Dorian colonists. The First Pythian thus becomes a *political* message: traditionalist, conservative, oligarchic, but of freedom.

Pindar hopes that Zeus will allow the destiny of the citizens and "kings" of this Sicilian city to be awarded "a true record on the lips of men": and that Hieron and Deinomenes, by "honoring" the people," will lead them to *hesychía*, to internal harmony and external peace, in particular regarding the Phoenicians and the Tyrrhenians—the Carthaginians and the Etruscans—who were defeated by Hieron, respectively, "by the well-watered bank of Himera" (480) and at Cumae (474). For Pindar, Hieron's victories in the west are in fact part of a single great series of events that freed all Greece from enslavement to the barbarians. In the fourth epode, the poet solemnly recalls the Athenians' victory over the Persians at Salamis (480) and the Spartans' in Platea (479), over Medes "with curved bows" (battles on land and sea, like Hieron's against Tyrrhenians and Phoenicians). Here, too, however, the celebration of that Panhellenic Nike is presented in an oblique manner: *while* he prays to Zeus to stop (on behalf of Syracuse) the "war cry" of Carthaginians and Etruscans, Pindar in reality addresses *himself*, declaring that Athens will be grateful to him, and that he will tell the "tale" of the Spartans' battle in Platea, "before Cithaeron"; and "by the well-watered bank of Himera" will complete the "song" (which in the third epode he had entreated the Muse to let him "sing" for Deinomenes alone) for the whole dynasty of the Deinomenides. In other words, Pindar proposes himself as a poet on the same level as the Greek victories in war: the victorious poet of all the Greeks.

Confirmation that the eagle is now looking at his own flight, at his own poetry, comes right afterward, in the fifth strophe, where Pindar articulates a poetics of measure, brevity, and compactness in complexity:

If you should speak in keeping with the occasion,

plaiting the threads of many matters into a brief whole,
men will find less fault with you;
for wearisome excess blunts the edge of keen expectancy,
and in their secret hearts men are especially oppressed
when they hear praise of other citizens.

The ideal is *opportunity*, understood both in the sense of dimension and in the sense of time: in the *First Nemean*, Pindar claims that he has touched the *kairós* of many things without spreading lies. Catching the right moment: everything has its due measure, and therefore it is best to recognize the *kairós*, what is "to the purpose." But "brief measure is, for men, the opportune moment," he declares. Now, finally, we understand why a Pindaric ode appears so varied, multiform, tense, colorful, compact: because the narration of the myths of Typhos and Philoctetes, the description of the eruption of Etna, and the allusions to contemporary history and Greece's ancestral roots are so concise and striking. Not only because men censure the man who is praised, get fed up with and envy him, which prevents the poet from elaborating his subjects at length, and compels him to choice and speed: but also because, like something that dominates and determines and accords with all that, the *kairós* that governs every thing is, for men, brief measure.

We have only a few true occasions, opportunities, moments. The poet has even fewer, because he has to find the appropriate correspondence in the event, in the athletic contest, in that moment, on that occasion: of due measure and to the point. The poet has to catch the *kairós* in the *kairós* and weave around this encounter a dense, multicolored tapestry; distill a liquid sweet as honey, pure and primordial as water; forge a lyre as shining and precious as gold.

In actions and in words, follow beauty, justice, and truth, Pindar exhorts Hieron at the end of the fifth strophe: "Do not deviate from your noble course. Steer your people with the rudder of justice, and forge your tongue on the anvil of truth." If a "spark," a triviality, leaps from the anvil it will seem great, because it comes from him, and "there are many men to bear reliable witness to your acts": may Hieron's words, like his works, be temperate, and his character—his state of mind—flourish and bear fruit in generosity. "If it pleases you to hear that men always speak well of you do not grow weary of spending." Renown is gained with munificence. So, Hieron, "like a steersman let your sail out to catch the wind": and so, like the sailors who set off with the favorable wind (of the second epode), you will have a good "return." And if those sailors who, at the moment of departure, were already thinking of the *nóstos*, the return, were, then, on the side of the founder of Etna and for the poet who celebrates him and looks at the aim— and at the end—of his own composition, now the return is the reward for Hieron's generosity, is, of course, the narrative and the poem that here and now join past and future, death and immortality.

The award of posthumous fame is the only testimony
that storytellers and poets can give to the lives of the dead.

Bards and *lógioi*: Pindar repeats it in the *Sixth Nemean*, combining the image of the archer who wants to hit the target and the invocation to the Muse. And if it seems strange that Pindar the bard, the embodiment of the poet-seer, associates storytellers with the praise and divine inspiration of the Muses, we should persuade ourselves that for him the storyteller, even in prose, of myths, and traditional stories (for example Hecataeus, a younger contemporary of Pindar and the author of *Stories* or *Genealogies* of this type) does work similar to his: Themistocles and Pausanias, the victors of Salamis and Platea, will have eternal fame, like Hieron's, thanks to the descendants of the *lógioi*, who have now become historians. Herodotus is about to enter the scene.

Furthermore, in the fifth epode, which ends the poem, the poet recalls two historical characters: Croesus, the immensely wealthy king of Lydia, whose "generous virtues," liberality and *pietas*, are everlasting (and with whom the *Histories* of Herodotus opens); and Phalaris, the tyrant of Agrigentum, whose ruthless mind invented the bronze bull in which he had his enemies roasted, and whose odious reputation endures, an "evil report throughout the world." The generous behavior and fair government that Pindar urges on Hieron have an illustrious precedent in Croesus, and poets and storytellers can celebrate both. Phalaris, instead, the negative example of treacherous tyranny, is destined to oblivion: "no lyres in men's halls welcome him to the soft embrace of boys' voices."

Thus at the end of the ode we have returned, in a perfect circle, to the spellbinding image of the opening, the golden lyre. Now, truly, the eagle ends its flight: on a peak, represented in life by the union of success and good reputation, joy in the present and fame in the future: "the man who lights on both and holds them fast wins *the highest crown.*"

How many circuits has the eagle made in its flight? Within the biggest one, from the lyre to the lyre, we now glimpse others, which are concentric: from the peace that the art of Apollo and the Muses spreads over Olympus to peace in the city of Etna and all Greece; from the rage of Typhos under the volcano to the barbarian Carthaginians, Etruscans, and Persians conquered on land and sea; from the prayer to Zeus and the proclamation of the Pythian victory of Hieron, in the second antistrophe, to another invocation to Zeus and the celebration of Hieron's victories at Cumae and Himera in the fourth antistrophe. Apollo and the Muses open the first strophe and return together at its end; Apollo is evoked again, implicitly, with the Muses, in the second epode; the Muse is invoked in the third. One could continue: words, images, figures, ideas—as we've seen repeatedly—correspond to one another, conflict, reprise, complete one another, as if we were in a Bach Fugue.

There was a plan in the eagle's flight: a supreme symmetry, a predicted order to be fulfilled, a harmony without equal. Not static, not sculptural: but in continuous rapid motion, re-creating itself. If we can see it now, in its entirety, from a fixed position, it's because Zeus' winged creature has finally come to rest on the "highest crown," and the dance and the song have ended. Now, in fact, we have fallen into sleep, into a torpor, into the *kóma* into which the golden lyre sinks men and gods, extinguishing even what shares the most rapid motion we know—the speed of light—and from eternity penetrates time: the lightning flash, the warlike bolt of ever-flowing fire. Now the eagle sleeps on Zeus' scepter, with folded wings, eyelids gently closed by the dark cloud of the music that pours over it, breathing the powerful and tranquil rhythm of sleep. *That*, too, is poetry: that is the experience we sometimes have of it.

The tremendous eruption of Etna, Philoctetes wounded and the victor over Troy, Hieron ruler of the West, the Persian wars, the origins and laws of the Dorians, Croesus and Phalaris—everything is now here. Ares, the god of *pólemos* and, as Heraclitus would say, of *éris*, of universal conflict, of the strife that dominates the cosmos, soothes his own heart for a moment, abandoning the sharp point of his spear; and all the gods are charmed by the poet's arrows and the strings of the lyre. Here where the javelin has been hurled and reached its goal, the farthest throw, and yet within the field: in the right place, at the right moment, at the fitting time, at Delphi or on Etna, where the ode is sung in the fifth century before our era; in Rome, Cambridge, or the Sabine Hills, when, in the twenty-first century, we pick it up again. Because the *kairós* is *in it*. It's here that the sea, the earth, the sky, and the abysses of the planet meet: eternal, past, present, and future; divine, chthonic, and human; myth, laws, history, and politics.

Chrýsea phórminx, the five tones—as at the beginning of the *First Olympian*—give voice to the world. Let's reread the strophe and antistrophe that open the First Pythian, silently, falling asleep.

Golden lyre, possession and colleague of Apollo and the violet-
haired Muses;
to you the dancer's step listens as it begins the bright celebration,
and the singers obey your directions when with quivering strings
you strike up the preludes which lead to the dance.
You stifle even the warlike thunderbolt of ever-flowing fire;
and the eagle, king of birds, sleeps on the scepter of Zeus,
folding his swift wings to his sides,
because you have poured a dark cloud over his bent head,
a sweet shutter for his eyelids;
in sleep he flexes his supple back, spellbound by your throbbing
music.
And violent Ares lays aside his cruelly pointed spear
and warms his heart in sleep,
for your shafts charm even the hearts of gods,
through the skill of Leto's son and the Muses with their deep-folded
robes.

In the profound torpor that has now seized us, we again
experience the great flight of the ode, we feel the force of
Zeus "Accomplisher," to whom we owe everything, we
hear his name repeated five times: he has defeated chaos by
burying Typhos, and rules over Olympus and over Etna.
Everything happens in his shadow: in his hand the light-
ning, on his scepter the eagle, as in the statue of Phidias in
Olympia. He is the *theós*, the God: to whom Pindar has
raised a famous Song and whom Aeschylus in his tragedies
celebrates as the Unique. The divine, then, invoked repeat-
edly by the poet, is an integral part of the poem, which
praises the divine, and, along with Zeus, the *sophía* of
Apollo and the song of the Muses dominate in the ode: the
wise art of the god who from birth has possessed the lyre,

the bow, and the oracles; and the melodious and terrible voice of the daughters of Memory. Recognizing that "all mortal achievement stems from the gods' designs"—wisdom, strength, word—means giving to god that which belongs to god: understanding that in the universe in general, as in this place and this moment, a full Being acts, transcendent but always immanent, unfathomably distant from man and yet very close to him.

But in the affairs of men, as in the Trojan War, there is still a *moiridion*, a fate, that is unfolding and coming to fulfillment over time, together with human action, with stringing the bow of Philoctetes, exhausted by his wound, with Hieron, who is ill, victorious in the race and in battles. As these threads are interwoven there is a point where they come together: the *kairós*, the occasion that is just, opportune, and proper. It will be the founding of Etna and its establishment of just laws, it will be the victories of Athens and Sparta over the Persians: the *kairós* is *in* history and *in* politics: and poetry sings these openly, without hiding, because it is itself the adaptation of words to the occasion. The events continually repeated in Pindar's poetry—the athletes' victories in the games—are transcended only as they come *to the point,* thanks to a skill that ascends, that soars: obsessed and measured, dark and luminous, clear as water and gleaming as gold.

But life, too, in Pindar's ideal, is clear as water and gleaming as gold, dark and luminous. An ethics of the beautiful, the just, and the true outlines its plan in the present, within the brief time conceded to mankind on earth: forgetfulness of sufferings first, then prosperity and abundance of riches; the honor that crowns wealth, and joy in success and a good reputation. When a man meets both and seizes them, or when you meet a man who seizes both, this is truly the supreme *critical point*: the *kairós* of life, the "highest crown." Then one can say that *cháris*—grace, beauty, splendor, favor—governs existence. And proclaim, as the *First Olympian* does, with the same brilliance and lightning flash of the *First Pythian*, victory for Hieron, this time in the chariot race:

Water is best,
while gold gleams like blazing fire in the night,
brightest amid a rich man's wealth.

Here, too, poetry immediately took possession of the primordial liquid and the golden splendor, aiming at sun and stars:

but, my heart, if it is of games that you wish to sing,
look no further than the sun: as there is no star
that shines with more warmth by day from a clear sky.

But note: poetry (like that type of life as well) isn't for everyone, in fact for some—for many—it's dangerous and terrible: "Creatures unloved by Zeus shudder when they hear the Pierians' voice, whether on earth or in the relentless sea." A "profound, unruly" terror overwhelms the enemies of God at the song of the Muses wherever they are in the world. And if, with Pindar, we should identify these beings with enemies of the Olympian order, with monsters like Typhos, we could always ask ourselves: why do those unloved by God tremble with fear when they hear poetry? Why for him or her does the voice of the Muses become a war cry? And what, exactly, is the *philía* of Zeus, the love of God? A deep unease grips us, people of the twenty-first century of the secular era: the love of God and our capacity to taste poetry, to be bewitched by it, are mysteriously bound together, as if we were talking about a biblical prophecy. Let's not ruin its delicate, precarious balance: we could find ourselves again—oh truly unbearable fate—shuddering at the music that charms the eagle and puts him to sleep. "Brief measure," let's remember, "is, for men, the opportune moment." "The cruellest thing, they say," the passage continues, "is to know the good but to be forced to stand apart from it."

IX
THE INVENTION OF ROME

It is precisely the element of the unexpected in the events I have cho-
sen to describe which will challenge and stimulate everyone alike,
both young and old, to study my systematic history. There can surely
be nobody so petty or so apathetic in his outlook that he has no
desire to discover by what means and under what system of govern-
ment the Romans succeeded in less than fifty-three years in bringing
under their rule almost the whole of the inhabited world, an achieve-
ment which is without parallel in human history. Or from the oppo-
site point of view, can there be anyone so completely absorbed in
other subjects of contemplation or study that he could find any task
more important than to acquire this knowledge?[37]

Polybius, opening of the *Histories*. Polybius is one of the
defeated of history, and one of the many defeated by Rome,
who became a hero of historiography. He was a Greek from
Arcadia, and the commander of the cavalry of the Achaean
League, when the Romans, right in the middle of the Punic
Wars, crushed Macedonia. He was taken hostage and trans-
ported to Rome, where he frequented the cultural circles of
Lucius Aemilius Paulus and the Scipiones. At that time he
began to write the history of Rome. Like many in the
ancient world and the modern, he wondered how a small
village of shepherds straddling the Tiber could in a short
time have become master of the world and how it was able

to remain so for such a long time. The empires that pre-
ceded Rome—Persia, Sparta, Macedonia—hadn't lasted so
long, or hadn't been so extensive as Rome. What distin-
guished Rome from all the others? Polybius answered that
the reason was the Roman "constitution," the fact that
Rome preserved in the form of its government essential
characteristics of monarchy, aristocratic government, and
democracy (the same is said today of the United States).

Rome was a unique venture not only in the ancient
world but, later, in the medieval and modern worlds.
Polybius wasn't the only one to make the observation.
Plutarch suggested that Fortune laid the city's foundation
and Valor built on it. Cicero extolled the intelligence that
presided over the choice of location: "As regards the site of
his city—a matter which calls for the most careful foresight
on the part of one who hopes to plant a commonwealth
that will endure—he [Romulus] made an incredibly wise
choice. For he did not build it down by the sea, though it
would have been very easy for him . . . to invade the terri-
tory of the Rutuli and the Aborigines, or he might have
founded his city on the mouth of the Tiber. . . . But with
remarkable foresight our founder perceived that a site on
the sea-coast is not the most desirable for cities founded in
the hope of long life and extended dominion."[38]

Other historians put military might first. How did the
Romans free themselves from the Etruscan superpower, for
example? They had the Etruscans in their house and right
outside: the last kings of Rome were Etruscan, as their
names testify, and the Etruscan city of Veii, which took
Rome ten years to conquer, today is on the periphery of

Rome itself. In order to defeat the Etruscans and the other populations of Italy, the Greeks of Magna Grecia, and the Carthaginians, the Romans armed themselves heavily and organized their armies efficiently, constructing roads, bridges, supply points, cities. Surely this is what sustained Rome as the head of the world for almost a thousand years.

Still others maintain that the secret of Rome lay in its inclusiveness and acceptance of "others," in the capacity for assimilation that led Caracalla, in 212 A.D., to extend Roman citizenship to all free inhabitants of the empire. Certain historians and poets had been aware of this for some time. Livy recounts that, soon after its founding, Rome was already so strong that it rivaled every neighboring population, but "because of the scarcity of women its greatness would endure only a generation." Then Romulus designed a perfect trick: he organized games in honor of Equestrian Neptune, ordering his messengers to spread the word among the neighboring populations. Drawn mainly by curiosity to see the new city, these populations thronged to the site: among them were the Sabines, with their children and wives. During the spectacle, a melee was deliberately incited, which offered the young Romans an opportunity to rush in and rape the women of the guests. Humiliated husbands and other relatives assembled under Titus Tatius to respond with force.

This is the Rape of the Sabine Women and the first of the Roman wars of the next millennium. But it's also an occasion to establish peace on a new basis, with a far-seeing politics of assimilation. According to the historians, in fact, Romulus and the Romans initially devoted themselves to flattering the women, promising them citizenship, goods, and progeny, and justifying their acts with the passion of love. Later, when the battle raged between Romans and Sabines, the women themselves intervened, peace was established, and of two peoples "a single one was made." Romulus and Titus Tatius ruled together, and the second king of Rome, the "pacific" Numa Pompilius, was of Sabine origin.

Even Virgil, the greatest poet of Rome, understands the extraordinary force of attraction that the Roman politics of welcome and tolerance exercises on other peoples. With the *Aeneid*, he composes for Augustus the great epic poem of Rome: the first half, inspired by the *Odyssey*, tells of Aeneas' wanderings; the second, in which Aeneas goes to war for the conquest of Lazio, is modeled on the *Iliad*. At the center of the poem, Virgil places Book VI, in which he celebrates a real apotheosis of Rome and, especially, the *gens julia*, to which Augustus belonged.

Guided by the Cumaean Sybil, Aeneas, like Odysseus before him, descends to the lower world. He meets the ferryman Charon and a crowd of unburied dead (including his helmsman Palinurus), and passes Acheron, Cerberus, Minos, the suicides, and the Fields of Mourning, to which those who suffered for love are assigned; among them is Dido, who refuses to speak to Aeneas. The glorious victims of the war, Trojans and Greeks, crowd around him. Then, avoiding the entrance to Tartarus, Aeneas and the Sybil reach the Elysian Fields, the home of the blessed. The poet Musaeus leads Aeneas to his father, Anchises.

In the conversation that follows, Anchises, answering a question from his son, illustrates the state of the souls and the changes in them, then leads him up to a height from which he can see them all. "My tongue will now reveal the fame that is to come from Dardan sons / and what Italian children wait for you—/ bright souls that are about to take your name; in them I shall unfold your fates." Here Aeneas is confronted by an array of figures who incarnate the legend of Rome, from his immediate descendants—Silvius, Procas, and Numitor—to the founder Romulus and, with a leap, Julius Caesar and Augustus:

"This is the man you heard so often promised—
Augustus Caesar, son of a god, who will
renew a golden age in Latium,
in fields where Saturn once was king, and stretch
his rule beyond the Garamantes and
the Indians—a land beyond the paths
of year and sun, beyond the constellations,
where on his shoulders heaven-holding Atlas
revolves the axis set with blazing stars."[39]

The exaltation of Augustus is at the center of the Triumph of Rome announced by Anchises. After him, the voice traverses the story of the city, returning to the successors of Romulus up to the end of the monarchy, and descending through the centuries of the republic by evoking Brutus, the Deci, the Drusi, Manlius Torquatus, Furius Camillus, Julius Caesar, Pompey, Lucius Mummius, Lucius Aemilius Paulus, Cato (Censor or Uticensis), Aulus Cornelius Cossus, the Gracchi, the Scipiones, Caius Baritius Luscinus, Serranus, the Fabii, until he reaches Marcus Claudius Marcellus, the adopted son and son-in-law of

Augustus, who would have been his heir but died. Just before pausing on Marcellus, Anchises proclaims openly the ideology by which Rome should be inspired:

"For other peoples will, I do not doubt,
still cast their bronze to breathe with softer features,
or draw out of the marble living lines,
plead causes better, trace the ways of heaven
with wands and tell the rising constellations;
but yours will be the rulership of nations,
remember, Roman, these will be your arts:
to teach the ways of peace to those you conquer,
to spare defeated peoples, tame the proud."

The Greeks may be better sculptors, orators, and astronomers than the Romans, but the latter will have to govern peoples, "teach the ways of peace," *parcere subiectis et debellare superbos.* Spare those who submit: assimilate them, make them Roman citizens. Defeat, exterminate, punish those who resist: along the road between Capua and Rome crucify five thousand rebel slaves, one after the other.

The Romans carried out this double task exceptionally well, despite the corruption that dominated their society and their political life, and despite the tremendous power struggles that divided them. They offered the world order, imposing a highly developed legal system and constructing, in the course of centuries, roads, bridges, aqueducts, baths, theaters, throughout Europe, the Middle East, and North Africa, in a manner unequaled before or after, up to the modern era.

For this reason, they also invented a legend of themselves

and their city that conditioned the Western imagination even after the decline of their hegemony. Horatii and Curiatii, Mucius Scaevola, Horatius Cocles, Furius Camillus, Cincinnatus are characters—whether historical or mythical doesn't matter—who for thousands of years represented an identity and an ethics. For the founding of the city, Roman poetry and history invented the legendary deeds of Alba Longa, of Numior and Amulius, of Mars and Rhea Silvia, of the wolf and the woodpecker, and the twins raised by the shepherds Faustulus and Acca Larentia, of the construction of Roma Quadrata on the Palatine, of the quarrel between Remus and Romulus, and the killing of the former.

Romans and Greeks collaborated in the mythopoiesis: some propose as founding fathers the descendants of the Trojan Aeneas, some instead attribute the founding to the heirs of Odysseus. Fabius Pictor and Hellanicus, Hesiod and Ennius, Virgil and Ovid, Livy, Dionysus of Halicarnassus, and Diodorus Siculus: all examined the origins, infancy, and development of Rome. And even many centuries later, when the city was losing its grandeur and its power, echoes of the legend resound in the last pagan writers and the Fathers of the Church: in Servius and the Vatican Mythographer, in Justinian, St. Jerome, and St. Augustine.

The invention of Rome is a subtle and complex matter, which perhaps could be said to have been completed in the first century B.C., after Polybius and after the historians of the republican age did their work. The Romans themselves are aware of it, and often make a point of boasting that in the wars fought against non-Romans fate would lead them first to disaster and then, later, save and exalt them. The same happens in the wars against the Italic peoples, the Etruscans, the Gauls (who went so far as to sack Rome), the Samnites, Pyrrhus and the Greeks of southern Italy, and, finally, the Carthaginians, in the Second Punic War. Often abandoned by their allies, the Romans recover from defeat thanks to a unique resilience, as Livy's account of the events of the Second Punic War—after Hannibal's invasion of Italy and up to the decision to take the war to Africa—demonstrates.

The Roman intellectuals are also conscious of the immense internal conflicts that mark the growth of the republic: between plebes and patricians, between opposing factions of the senatorial order. In the transformation from a small city-state, based on "an Italic economic social arrangement of small peasant landowners," into the capital of an imperial republic extending over the entire Mediterranean, the old equilibrium, which, according to Cicero, led Scipio Aemilianus to speak of a *res populi*, breaks down. The conquests involve enormous revenues, the development of a direct administration, innumerable masses of new slaves and therefore a free workforce, the formation of great landed properties, and, naturally, contact with various cultural traditions. Cicero wrote a *Concordia ordinum* that promoted harmony between the senatorial and equestrian classes, and, later, amplified this idea in the *Consensus omnium bonorum*. In the end, the mere establishment of the Augustan Principate led to the creation of a new equilibrium.

In the meantime, the republic had been ruined by personal ambition, corruption, misuse of public funds, secret accords between individuals or groups. One has only to read Cicero's orations against Verres—a man who dissipated the treasury, subjected Asia and Pamphylia to harassments, as an urban praetor administered justice like a brigand, reduced Sicily to total ruin—to understand what sort of phenomena we're talking about.

Or turn to Sallust, who devotes the opening chapters of his *The War with Catiline*[40] to a reconstruction of the moral degradation of Rome. First, he writes, came ambition, among noble and ignoble alike, the latter advancing it by cheating and lying. Then greed, the passion for money: after a good beginning, Sulla plunged Rome into crime, and "all men began to rob and pillage; one coveted a house, another lands; the victors showed neither moderation nor restraint, but did shameful and cruel deeds against their fellow citizens." Sulla allowed the army to live in luxury in order to insure its loyalty. The Roman soldiers learned then "to indulge in women and wine; to admire statues, paintings, and chased vessels; to steal them from private houses and public places; to pillage shrines, and to desecrate everything, both sacred and profane. . . . [They] left nothing to the vanquished." If that's what was happening in the subject territories, its effects can be imagined in Italy: theft, dissipation, disdain for laws human and divine, stealing from allies, a craving for sex, food, luxury.

Augustus attempted to rebuild Rome not only architecturally but also morally: it was in effect a "reinvention," and Virgil was its principal (but not only) officiant. The problem is that the Augustan ideal proclaimed by Virgil was extremely high and easily collapsed at the first contact with reality. And reality itself changed not long after Augustus' death: the empire, passing into the hands of his Julian-Claudian successors—Tiberius, Caligula, Claudius, and Nero—was inevitably transformed by character of each and by altered political conditions. Reading Tacitus and Suetonius, who in a different form reconstructed the history of first-century Rome through the reign of Domitian—a period when the empire continued to prosper and expand and then was halted (the conquest of Britain took place under Claudius, the invasion of Germany ended after the defeat of Teutoburg)—we seem to be present, when it comes to imperial personalities (with the exception of Vespasian and Titus), at a progressive deterioration of mental and psychic conditions, an increasingly oppressive tyranny, a rise in capriciousness, criminality, and cruelty.

So much so that Tacitus, the greatest of the Latin historians, finds it necessary to begin his *Annals* with the promise that he will confront the subject *sine ira et studio*, "without anger or favor,"[41] thus avoiding the fearfulness with which the acts of those emperors had been narrated while they were alive, and the hatred after they were dead. In the two preceding works, however, the *Agricola* and the *Histories* (dedicated to the three emperors during the year following the death of Nero, and then the Flavians), Tacitus had had a different attitude. Every word expressed horror at the rule of Domitian. Julius Agricola, his father-in-law, who died prematurely, didn't get to live until "the light of this happy age, and to see Trajan ruling," but at least he was spared "those last days wherein Domitian no longer fitfully and with breathing spaces, but with one continuous and, so to speak, single blow, poured forth the life-blood of the state."[42]

Nero after all withdrew his eyes, nor contemplated the crimes he authorized. Under Domitian it was no small part of our sufferings that we saw him and were seen of him; that our sighs were counted in his books; that not a pale cheek of all that company escaped those brutal eyes, that crimson face which flushed continually lest shame should unawares surprise it.

In the *Histories* Tacitus admits that he has received help in his career from the Flavians: "I would not deny that my elevation was begun by Vespasian," he writes, "augmented by Titus, and still further advanced by Domitian."[43] But someone who is loyal without being corrupt shouldn't paint portraits with affection or with hatred (*neque amore et sine odio*). For once, Tacitus finds himself with the "rare happiness of times when we may think what we please, and express what we think." Thus here is the picture of Rome at the end of Domitian's reign:

In the capital there were yet worse horrors. Nobility, wealth, the refusal or the acceptance of office, were grounds for accusation, and virtue ensured destruction. The rewards of the informers were no less odious than their crimes; for while some seized on consul-ships and priestly offices as their share of the spoil, others on procuratorships, and posts of more confidential authority, they robbed and ruined in every direction amid universal hatred and ter-ror. Slaves were bribed to turn against their masters, and freedmen to betray their patrons; and those who had not an enemy were destroyed by friends.

To find a similar situation we have to go back to Nero, as Tacitus does in the *Annals*. The story of Nero's suppression of Piso's plot, for example, unfolds before our eyes like a series of scenes from Shakespeare's *Richard III*: in two years, between 65 and 66, dozens of people, in addition to the cream of the *intelligentsia* of the time—which includes Lucan, Petronius, and Seneca—are killed or forced to suicide. The forced suicide of Seneca (who probably wasn't even implicated in the plot) is narrated by Tacitus with a coldness that reveals its pathos. Receiving the order to kill himself, the old Seneca asks the centurion who delivered it if he can consult his own will. When permission is denied, he reproaches his friends for their grief and imparts a last lesson in thought and Stoic ethics, while he accuses the emperor: "Who is not familiar with Nero's brutality? Nothing remains after murdered mother and brother but to add the slaughter of teacher and guide to the heap!" Seneca and his wife, Paulina, cut their veins. Nero has Paulina saved, so as not to increase "the odiousness of his ferocity." But Seneca's veins don't produce enough blood, so he begs one of his friends to give him the hemlock, which has long since been prepared—the same poison used to kill Socrates. But that isn't effective, either: the philosopher's limbs are cold and his body is insensitive to the action of the liquid. Then Seneca gets in a tub of hot water and, "sprinkling the nearest slaves, added: 'This liquid is a libation to Jupiter Liberator.'" Finally, he's carried to a steam bath and dies, suffocating.

It's a horror story, as an old body, though ravaged by suffering, refuses to die, and yet Seneca bears this torture patiently, almost lightly. If this death hadn't been typically Stoic, and weren't a suicide, it might be seen as similar to the Passion of Christ. No one knows if Tacitus was familiar with the narratives of the Christian Gospels, but his account of the death of Seneca, in the *Annals*, comes only twenty chapters after the description of Nero's persecution of the Christians, following the fire that destroyed most of the center of Rome in July of 64. To halt the rumor according to which the fire was "ordered," Nero laid the blame on "people popularly called Christians, hated for their perversions," subjecting them to "elaborate punishments." It's the first mention of the new religion in the writings of a Latin author:

The name's source was one Christus, executed by the governor Pontius Pilate when Tiberius held power. The pernicious creed, suppressed at the time, was bursting forth again, not only in Judaea, where this evil originated, but even in Rome, in which from all directions everything appalling and shameful flows and foregathers. At first, those who confessed were arrested. Then, on their evidence, a huge multitude was convicted, less for the crime of fire than for hatred of humankind. Their deaths were accompanied by derision: covered in animal skins they were to perish torn by dogs, or affixed to crosses to be burnt for nocturnal illumination when light faded. Nero offered his park for the show and staged games in the Circus, mixing with the crowd in the garb of a driver or riding a chariot. This roused pity. Guilty and deserving of extreme measures though they were, the Christians' annihilation seemed to arise not from public utility but for one man's brutality.

Tacitus has no sympathy for the Christians and shares the incomprehension and the prejudices of his contemporaries toward them. And though he reports their torture in all its crudeness and cruelty, he ignores any notion of martyrdom, and in fact points out that the first to be arrested, confessed Christians, denounced others. But he records the birth of compassion among the inhabitants of Rome. Presumably this pity (*miseratio*) is what will lead the Romans to approach the new religion and convert to it in numbers that, despite the persecutions, continue to grow.

The image of the Christians forced to wear animal skins in order to be torn to pieces by dogs, or crucified in order to burn like nocturnal torches in the imperial park, while Nero goes around the Circus dressed as a charioteer, is so emblematically powerful that it gives sudden and unexpected physicality to the *debellare superbos* of the *Aeneid*. Equally strong are Tacitus' attacks on the *parcere subiectis* and all the imperial ideology. In the *Agricola*, where he recounts the conquest of Britain by his father-in-law, he pauses on an episode that has become very famous. We are in Scotland, on the Mons Graupius, where the Britons have prepared the last resistance against the Romans: thirty thousand fighters, all the young and "the old still healthy and vigorous," as Tacitus writes, imitating the Virgilian portrait of Charon. One of the barbarian leaders, Calgacus, addresses the Britannic troops with a great speech, exhorting them to fight to preserve the island's freedom. Up to now, Calgacus says, we, who "dwell on the uttermost confines of the earth and of freedom," have been defended by our very isolation and by being largely unknown. Now "the uttermost parts of Britain lie exposed." For the Romans, everything that is unknown is grand, but we have nothing anymore but the waves and the rocks and "the yet more terrible Romans, from whose oppression escape is vainly sought by obedience and submission." Spare those who submit, as Anchises preached? Don't even mention it! The Romans are nothing but *raptores orbis*, robbers of the world:

Robbers of the world, now that earth fails their all-devastating hands, they probe even the sea: if their enemy have wealth, they have greed; if he be poor, they are ambitious; East nor West has glutted them; alone of mankind they covet with the same passion want as much as wealth. To plunder, butcher, steal, these things they misname empire: they make a desolation and they call it peace. (*auferre trucidare rapere falsis nominibus imperium, atque ubi solitudinem faciunt, pacem appellant.*)

"Teach the ways of peace," Anchises said in the *Aeneid*. But that "peace," Calgacus claims, is the wasteland made by the Romans in the lands they've conquered! On the other hand, Tacitus in the *Annals* records the story of another rebel British chieftain, Caratacus, who was captured by the Romans and brought to Rome, where he made such an impressive speech before the emperor, appealing to his "clemency," that he was pardoned and allowed to live in peace in the city. Finally, in the *Histories* Tacitus himself constructs the speech that Petilius Cerialis, a general who fought against Queen Boudicca and eventually became governor of Britannia, made to the Treveri and Lingones. What he said, in effect, was that Roman dominion is necessary to establish peace. Gaul had always been deeply divided by internal wars, until it yielded to Rome. Cerialis in fact offers a typical argument in favor of Roman domination: "We, though so often provoked, have used the right of conquest to burden you only with the cost of maintaining peace. For the tranquillity of nations cannot be preserved without armies; armies cannot exist without pay; pay cannot be furnished without tribute; all else is common between us. You often command our legions. You rule these and other provinces. There is no privilege, no exclusion. From worthy Emperors you derive equal advantage, though you dwell so far away, while cruel rulers are most formidable to their neighbours." Should the Romans be driven out, Cerialis adds, there would be immediate chaos and war, and the *subiecti*, who have gold and wealth, would suffer most. "By the prosperity and order of eight hundred years has this fabric of empire been consolidated, nor can it be overthrown without destroying those who overthrow it. . . . Give therefore your love and respect to the cause of peace, and to that capital in which we, conquerors and conquered, claim an equal right. Let the lessons of fortune in both its forms teach you not to prefer rebellion and ruin to submission and safety." Peace justifies empire.

The conflict between Arminius and his brother Flavus—one the leader of the Germans who defeated the Romans in the battle of Teutoburg, the other a soldier in the Roman army—stands out in the *Annals* and, as far as Arminius is concerned, seems to go in the same direction as Calgacus:

Flavus' [speech] was on Rome's greatness, Germanicus' resources. For the defeated, punishments are severe, for anyone surrendering, there is ready mercy. Your wife and son are not treated as enemies. Arminius' [speech] was on duty to country, the liberty they inherited, Germany's household gods, their mother his ally in entreaty. Do not choose being the deserter and betrayer of friends and kinfolk, indeed of your own people, over being their ruler.

The two brothers gradually descend to insults and would have started fighting if they hadn't been separated by their men and the Weser river. In fact, they embody, dramatically, two worlds: the Romanized barbarian, who has fully absorbed the Virgilian ideology (Flavus is a soldier in Germanicus' army), and the barbarian who, having experienced Romanization, violently rejects it and returns to his roots to prepare the resistance.

The anti-Roman speech of the barbarian leader is a standard of Roman historical literature. In the *Gallic Wars*, Julius Caesar has Critognatus speak before the final battle in Alesia. He urges the Gauls to unite in the resistance against Rome, citing as examples the fight against the Cimbri and the Teutones:

For in what was that war like this? The Cimbri, after laying Gaul waste, and inflicting great calamities, at length departed from our country, and sought other lands; they left us our rights, laws, lands, and liberty. But what other motive or wish have the Romans, than, induced by envy, to settle in the lands and states of those whom they have learned by fame to be noble and powerful in war, and impose on them perpetual slavery? For they never have carried on wars on any other terms. But if you know not these things which are going on in distant countries, look to the neighboring Gaul, which being reduced to the form of a province, stripped of its rights and laws, and subjected to Roman despotism, is oppressed by perpetual slavery.[44]

Caesar uses Critognatus' speech to make the war in Gaul appear to be a clash between civilization and the barbarians, as Critognatus goes so far as to defend the cannibalism of his ancestors, which was practiced on old people no longer fit for combat, during the war against the Cimbri and the Teutones. But the anti-Roman motivations are always clear: choosing surrender to Rome means choosing perpetual slavery, suffering the fate of Provence.

Sallust is even harsher. In the *War with Jugurtha*, Jugurtha addresses his father-in-law Bocchus, the ally who later delivers him to the Romans, in a speech that the historian summarizes like this: "The Romans, he said, were unjust, of boundless greed, and the common foes of all mankind; they, to whom all monarchies are adversaries, had the same motive for war with Bocchus as with himself and other nations, namely, the lust for dominion. At that moment, he, Jugurtha, was the Romans' enemy; a short while ago it had been the Carthaginians and King Perses; in the future it would be whoever seemed to them most prosperous."

But it is in the letter that Mithridates sends to Arsaces to induce him to form an alliance against Rome that Sallust, who inserted it into Book IV of his *Histories*, shows fully what the "proud men" of Virgil must have thought of Roman domination. Mithridates lingers on the causes and developments of the conflict that he has fought against Rome, stating, "In fact, the Romans have one inveterate motive for making war upon all nations, peoples and kings; namely, a deep-seated desire for dominion and for riches." For this reason they fought and conquered or tricked Philip V of Macedonia, and later Antiochus III of Syria, Perseus the son of Philip, Eumenes of Pergamum, Nicomedes of Bithynia—in short, in only fifty-three years, as Polybius said, they became masters of the world. It's good to know what the "empire" of Rome means, Mithridates continues:

"Or are you not aware that the Romans turned their arms in this direction only after Ocean put an end to their westward progress? That from the beginning they have possessed nothing except what they have stolen: their homes, wives, lands, and dominion? That having been once upon a time refugees without a native land or parents, they have been established to serve as a plague upon the whole world, being men who are prevented by nothing human or divine from plundering and destroying allies and friends—those situated far away or nearby, weak and powerful too—and from considering as their enemies all powers not subservient to them and especially monarchies. . . . The Romans have weapons against all men, the sharpest against those from whom conquest yields the greatest spoils; they have grown mighty by audacity and deceit and by sowing wars from wars. In keeping with this custom, they will destroy everything, or they will perish in the attempt."[45]

The accusation, both in Sallust and in Tacitus (who certainly was aware of his predecessor), is the same: what the Romans call "empire" is, as Calgacus says better than all, robbery, slaughter, plunder. It is a matter not of governing peoples, as Anchises maintains in the *Aeneid*, but of conquering them, dominating them, robbing them. It's not empire: it's imperialism. But maybe it should be noted that the vigorous anti-imperialism to which the non-Romans of Caesar, Sallust, and Tacitus give voice is, after all, a creation of Roman intellectuals. Also in this Rome invented: not only itself but the entire West to come.

X
EVERYTHING CHANGES, NOTHING DIES

Of bodies changed to other forms I tell;
You Gods, who have yourselves wrought every change,
Inspire my enterprise and lead my lay
In one continuous song from nature's first
Remote beginnings to our modern times.

Ere land and sea and the all-covering sky
Were made, in the whole world the countenance
Of nature was the same, all one, well named
Chaos, a raw and undivided mass,
Naught but a lifeless bulk, with warring seeds
Of ill-joined elements compressed together.
No sun as yet poured light upon the world,
No waxing moon her crescent filled anew,
Nor in the ambient air yet hung the earth,
Self-balanced, equipoised, nor Ocean's arms
Embraced the long far margin of the land.
Though there were land and sea and air, the land
No foot could tread, no creature swim the sea,
The air was lightless; nothing kept its form,
All objects were at odds, since in one mass
Cold essence fought with hot, and moist with dry,
And hard with soft and light with things of weight.
This strife a god, with nature's blessing, solved.[46]

This is the beginning of Ovid's *Metamorphoses*: with

Virgil's *Aeneid,* it's the greatest poem that Rome left us. While Virgil constructs a monument to the history and legend of the city, and, naturally, to the Julian dynasty—above all Augustus—Ovid, although at the end of the *Metamorphoses* he, too, celebrates Julius Caesar and Octavian Augustus, creates a completely different narrative: which, after the shortest and densest proem of all ancient literature, begins with the beginning of the world.

Describing the changing of "bodies" to "other forms" is the task that Ovid sets himself from the opening of his book: celebrating them in what he calls a *carmen perpetuum*, a continuous poem that goes from the beginning of the world up until his own day, with an unusual extension through time, and with the same velocity with which he announces it in the proem. Ovid's story of the beginning of the cosmos has illustrious precedents: Hesiod, Lucretius, and Virgil in poetry, and the pre-Socratics and Plato in philosophy. Although he preserves features derived from these authors, he innovates in a radical way. He chooses, in the first place, to paint a series of absences (no Sun, no Moon) rather than presences, and to concentrate attention on Chaos, avoiding any sort of theogony like Hesiod's, and taking up instead the primordial disorder of Lucretius. There is no Eros here that rules over other primeval divinities but, instead, "seeds of ill-joined elements": a formidable lack of equilibrium, of stability, which anticipates the perpetual changing of forms in the future—"Nothing kept its form."

Before "things"—or elements represented by land, sea, and sky—nature everywhere showed a uniform face: it was a "raw and undivided" mass, an inert, sluggish weight, that is, Chaos. Suddenly, the reader becomes aware of Ovid's choice of words, and the effort it must have taken to concentrate them into three lines: to concentrate *rudis indigestaque moles* (raw and undivided mass) and *pondus iners* (inert weight) and then *congestaque* (added to *indigesta*) *non bene iunctarum rerum discordia semina* (warring seeds of ill-joined elements compressed together).

In contrast with this tremendous capacity for synthesis, the next lines open up to absence, suspension, continuous change, and land finally on "strife," the clash of all the opposites, one against the other: cold and hot, moist and dry, soft and hard, heavy and light. When, finally, the god (*deus et melior natura*) takes a hand to the cosmos, his first action is to settle this conflict, separating—as the God of Genesis does—land from sky, waves from land, and each thing "he fastened in its place Appropriate in peace and harmony." Then he lights "in heaven's vault . . . the fiery weightless force," the Sun; next in lightness is air; then, burdened by the heavy elements, earth; finally water flows to the farthest corners. The god rounds the earth into a huge globe:

> then bade the sea
> Extend and rise under the rushing winds,
> And gird the shores of the encircled earth.
> Springs too he made and boundless fens and lakes,
> And rivers hemmed in winding banks to flow,
> Which, in their diverse journeyings, sometimes
> The earth absorbs, sometimes they reach the sea
> And in its broad domain, instead of banks,
> With new-found freedom beat upon the shores.

He bade the plains spread wide, the valleys sink,
The craggy mountains rise, the forest trees
Don their green leaves.

Gradually the world takes shape, becoming landscape
and geography, then history: the globe is divided into zones
according to climate, the winds blow from the four cardi-
nal points, the ether is spread, clear and pure, over them,
and, emerging from fog, the stars light up brilliantly for the
first time (the original has the beautiful *effervescere*) in the
sky. The universe fills with living beings: in the firmament
the stars, "the gods and goddesses," and the constellations;
the "shining" fish in the sea, the beasts on the land, the
birds in the air.

Man is born last, "made, perhaps from seed divine /
Formed by the great Creator, so to found / A better world,
perhaps the new-made earth, / So lately parted from the
ethereal heavens, / Kept still some essence of the kindred
sky—Earth that Prometheus molded, mixed with water, /
In likeness of the gods that govern the world." Formed by
the god, who is the *opifex rerum*, or shaped by Prometheus
"in likeness," as in the Bible, of divinity, the human being,
the "noblest" animal, a "holier creature" and "of a loftier
mind," doesn't look at the ground like the other animals but
holds his head up so that he can raise his eyes to the stars.

Now a "mythical story" of humankind can begin: the four
Ages, descending rapidly from the golden age to the iron; the
battle between Jove and the Giants; the council of gods and
the decision to exterminate man; the story of Lycaon, who
serves Jupiter a meal of human flesh, after which Jupiter

destroys his house and transforms him into a wolf. The exter-
mination of the human race is accomplished by a flood,
which only Deucalion and his wife, Pyrrha, survive, because
of their piety. The two obey the command of Themis to throw
behind them the bones of the ancient mother, and so they
cast behind them rocks they find on the ground; from these
a new human race is born, while from the mud of the flood
the animals resume their forms and terrible monsters come
into the world. One of these, the serpent-dragon Python,
who oversees Delphi, is killed by Apollo. This offends Cupid,
and he takes revenge by shooting an arrow that causes Apollo
to fall in love with the nymph Daphne. She rejects the god
and flees, pursued by him: when he is about to catch her, she
is transformed into a laurel.

This is one of the most beautiful moments of Book I and
of all the *Metamorphoses*. First the mad love of Apollo,
which burns like stubble in the fields, and then his contem-
plation of Daphne's body, her hair, her eyes like stars, her
lips, her fingers, hands, wrists, arms. While he follows her,
the god boasts about himself to her: he's not some ordinary
man, he's the son of Jupiter, the lord of Delphi, it's he who
reveals "things future, past, and present," who presides
over song and medicine. In vain: Daphne flees without
responding: the breeze bares her limbs, her dress flutters,
the light wind pushes back her hair. Like a hare pursued by
a hound, which opens its jaws believing it has caught its
prey, but the prey escapes, just grazing its teeth: so Daphne
and Apollo. Until, now caught, she invokes the aid of her
father, the river Peneus:

Scarce had she made her prayer when through her limbs
A dragging languor spread, her tender bosom
Was wrapped in thin smooth bark, her slender arms
Were changed to branches and her hair to leaves;
Her feet but now so swift were anchored fast
In numb stiff roots, her face and head became
The crown of a green tree; all that remained
Of Daphne was her shining loveliness.

Daphne has become a tree, which from now on will belong to Apollo, and whose leaves will crown the Roman poets and leaders. The laurel retains the *nitor*, the shining splendor of the body that was the nymph's. "Between seriousness and frivolity, between participation and irony, between Greek and Roman, between religion and individualism, between moral sense and cruelty, between nature and art": all the "vivid contrasts" that, according to the Italian classicist Alessandro Barchiesi, dominate the story culminate and vanish in this splendor, the stroke of genius that in half a line concludes a story narrated in little more than a hundred hexameters.

Allusivity, lightness, precision: the eroticism of the body undressed by the wind, that body transformed, limb by limb, into bark, leaves, branches, roots—flight transformed into the everlasting immobility of the plant. And afterward not a moment's respite. From this story another emerges: in the forest where Peneus rushes down from the mountain all the local rivers assemble, except Inacus, who has just lost his daughter Io. Immediately Ovid begins to narrate the story of Io: then, after Jupiter has transformed the nymph into a heifer, because of Juno's suspicions, and the heifer is given by the goddess to the monster with a hundred eyes, Argos, Ovid begins the story of the killing of Argos by Mercury, who has been sent by Jupiter.

To kill the monster Mercury casts a spell on him, putting him to sleep, by telling the story of the nymph Syrinx, a follower of Diana whom Pan falls in love with, and who, to escape him, is transformed into the Pan pipe. The poet naturally takes a detour in her direction, too, and returns to Io and Juno only at the end, when the goddess drives the heifer mad, and she wanders through the world until she reaches the shores of the Nile. Jupiter, who in the meantime has reconciled with Juno, restores human features to Io, who is worshiped as a goddess in Egypt. The son that Jupiter fathered with her, Epaphus, grows up with Phaeton, but the two quarrel precisely over the question of their fathers, Jupiter and Apollo. Phaeton, whose mother assures him about his paternity, hurries to his father, the Sun. And here ends Book I of the *Metamorphoses*; Book II opens with the story of Phaeton.

The pace of the *Metamorphoses* corresponds to its theme: meandering, undulating, changing—metamorphic. "Everything flows," Heraclitus had said, presumably, predicting the future. The *Metamorphoses* is the poem of becoming. Everything in it changes, from the cosmos of origins to the gods, from the bodies of human beings to those of the beasts, from flowers to the sea. In Ovid's poem the stories of animals that become stones, of heroes and nymphs changed into stars, gods that take human form originate in one another, intertwine, re-emerge in rapid sequence. One after the other, some two hundred and fifty of them strung together, they form a universal mythological story narrated from the point of view of change itself; at the same time, removed from the original frame, they constitute a summation of classical myth, a sort of encyclopedia of the most famous stories of antiquity, which dominated not only narrative in all Europe but also the visual art of the entire West: painting, sculpture, illumination.

This success would not have been possible without four fundamental elements: the concentration in the stories of all the passions and sufferings that rule the earthly world of men and women; the supremely economical style of the narrative, epitomized in the lightness, exactitude, visibility, and multiplicity that in Calvino's view made it a work for the third millennium; the inexhaustible energy that emanates from the whole; and the capacity to adapt to, or enter into, the interpretative criteria of various eras.

We have only to read a couple of the most famous stories to be aware of these qualities. I've chosen the stories of Echo and Narcissus and of Ceyx and Alcyone. The myth of Echo and Narcissus is the first episode of the *Metamorphoses* that deals with the love of humans. It begins, in Book III of the poem, with the prophecy that Tiresias utters over the newborn Narcissus, when his mother, the nymph Liriope, asks the prophet if the child will reach old age: *Si se non noverit*, if he doesn't know himself. The story plays ironically on this overturning of the Delphic oracle, which imposed on men *gnothi seauton: nosce te ipsum*, "Know thyself." At sixteen, Narcissus "seemed both boy and man," and is desired by many boys and many girls. He is harsh, and refuses all proposals, while he goes hunting deer.

Echo, "the nymph made of voice," is mad about Narcissus. Echo had concealed Jupiter's furtive love affairs with other nymphs, keeping Juno distracted by talk. At a certain point, the goddess realized this and punished Echo by taking away her capacity to speak, leaving her able only to echo the end of a sentence. Echo is hopelessly in love with Narcissus; secretly she follows him through the woods, burning with the desire to accost him with sweet words. But she can't: the only thing she can do is repeat his words:

It chanced Narcissus, searching for his friends,
Called "Anyone here?" and Echo answered "Here!"
Amazed he looked all round and, raising his voice,
Called "Come this way!" and Echo called "This way!"
He looked behind and, no one coming, shouted
"Why run away?" and heard his words again.
He stopped and, cheated by the answering voice,
Called "Join me here!" and she, never more glad
To give her answer, answered "Join me here!'
And graced her words and ran out from the wood
To throw her longing arms around his neck.
He bolted, shouting "Keep your arms from me!
Be off! I'll die before I yield to you."
And all she answered was "yield to you."
Shamed and rejected in the woods she hides
And has her dwelling in the lonely caves;
Yet still her love endures and grows on grief,
And weeping vigils waste her frame away;
Her body shrivels, all its moisture dries;
Only her voice and bones are left; at last
Only her voice, her bones are turned to stone.
So in the woods she hides and hills around,
For all to hear, alive, but just a sound.

For love of Narcissus Echo reduces herself to an echo: in the first metamorphosis of the episode, her body is consumed, and only voice and bones are left: when her bones turn to stone, only the sound amid the rocks remains. In the meantime, Narcissus continues to despise boys and girls, until a humiliated and exasperated youth invokes the punishment of Nemesis: "So may he love—and never win his love!"

One day, exhausted by the hunt and the heat, Narcissus lies down in the grass that surrounds a marvelous pool, "limpid and silvery," untouched by shepherds or animals, and sheltered by the forest from the sun's rays. Thirsty, he drinks some water. A beautiful reflection appears to him, and he loses his head: he falls in love with a shadow that has no body: he thinks it's a body but it's only water. Amazed by himself, he stares motionless at the face that is his. Lying on the ground "like a marble statue," he contemplates the stars of those reflected eyes, gazes, spellbound, at the hair, the cheeks, the mouth, the neck, "all he admires that all admire in him":

Himself he longs for, longs unwittingly,
Praising is praised, desiring is desired,
And love he kindles while with love he burns.
How often in vain he kissed the cheating pool
And in the water sank his arms to clasp
The neck he saw, but could not clasp himself!
Not knowing what he sees, he adores the sight;
That false face fools and fuels his delight.
You simple boy, why strive in vain to catch
A fleeting image? What you see is nowhere;
And what you love—but turn away—you lose!
You see a phantom of a mirrored shape;

Nothing itself; with you it came and stays;
With you it too will go, if you can go!

Narcissus is hopelessly in love with himself: but just as Echo before was condemned not to be loved by him, not to hold him and yield to him, so he is now condemned not to be able to clasp the image the water shows him, not to be loved in return, not to possess. He still doesn't know what he sees, but he burns for it. Finally, as he entreats the other he sees in the fountain, as he gives voice to his passion, he recognizes himself: *Iste ego sum! Sensi, nec me mea fallit imago ...:* "Oh, I am he! Oh, now I know for sure. The image is my own; it's for myself I burn with love; I fan the flames I feel."

He fulfills the prophecy that Tiresias had made to his mother, warning her: he knows himself. Immediately, then, he has presentiments of death: which doesn't trouble him, he says, but he would like the other to live longer. Impossible: "But now we two—one soul—one death will die." Again he is delirious, and he weeps. His tears ripple the water of the fountain, the apparition is obscured. When the water is calm again, and he sees in it his chest reddened by his own fists, he can't hold out any longer: "But as wax melts before a gentle fire, Or morning frosts beneath the rising sun," Narcissus is overcome, "wasted" by love, consumed by a hidden fire. Echo is present, invisible: although she is still bitter at the memory, she is gripped by sorrow. Every time he sobs, she responds with a sob; when he cries "farewell," she repeats "farewell." Worn out, Narcissus drops his head on the grass, and death closes his eyes, which are still fixed on the reflection. In Hades, he sees his reflection again, in the Styx. The Naiads and Dryads weep for him, but as the funeral rites are to take place, his body can't be found: in its place is a flower, white petals around a saffron center: the narcissus.

An almost pre-Baroque story, made up of spirals, contrasts, retaliations, echoes. Sound and gaze, first, then, in sequence, sound alone, gaze, and sound until the farewell, and the final gaze, in the Styx. A double narrative, interwoven, like an echo of itself, each part leading to the consumption of a body: the first dissolved in the air, amid rocks and forests, the other vanishing after death, replaced by a flower. Two types of love, one open and ready to yield, the other closed in itself: extreme, incapable of drawing any lesson from the knowledge it arrives at—narcissistic, there's no doubt, or pre-narcissistic, in the sense that the image of self is, in the narrative, ostensibly external, while the desire is all internal. In any case, it's a powerful, fascinating story, irreparably tragic and infinitely sad: one might be tempted to call it a story that has not yet used up its echo.

The stories of the *Metamorphoses* are all unhappy. There are no happy events as such in the poem, except when the metamorphosis takes place in the sky, that is, when a nymph who is loved and dies or is killed on the earth is transformed into a constellation or a star. There are, on the other hand, a number of consoling conclusions.

An example of these is the story of Ceyx and Alcyone, in Book XI, which takes us back unexpectedly to Alcman—at least six centuries before Ovid—and his poem about the halcyons and the kingfisher. Alcman had imagined, as we saw in Chapter 8, that as an old man the kingfisher has himself transported by the female "over the foaming brine." Ovid goes much farther. Alcyone, the daughter of the king of the winds, has married Ceyx, the king of Trachis, in Thessaly, and the son of Lucifer, the morning star. Ceyx decides to go and consult an oracle. Alcyone tries to dissuade him: she's afraid of the sea, of the "broken timbers" of shipwrecks she's seen on the beach, of the empty tombs bearing the names of the drowned. Not even Aeolus, her father, would be able to save her husband: once unleashed, the winds possess the sea and can sweep away everything. If Ceyx really wants to go, at least take her with him. Ceyx, though moved by her words and burning with love, doesn't want to give up the journey or expose her to the dangers of the crossing. He swears that he will return in two months, and embarks. Alcyone, shuddering, watches his figure as it grows indistinguishable, then the boat, and finally the sail. When that, too, vanishes, she rushes in anguish to her room and throws herself on the bed, weeping desperately.

Meanwhile Ceyx and his men continue the journey. But a tremendous storm approaches and hits the boat. Ovid describes the hurricane at length, with frightening precision, shifting his camera from the details—gestures, movements, words of the sailors—to a shadowy view of the elements in turmoil. "Sea piles on sea as if to reach the sky, The hanging pall of clouds is wet with spray. Here the waves take the colour of the sand, Swept from the deep, here black as Styx they swirl, There flat and white they hiss in sheets of foam." The waves crash against the ship, each more powerful and devastating than the last; night and storm envelope everything in darkness torn by lightning flashes, while the men, who first seek to pull in the sails and bail water, are now in the grip of panic: some weep, some pray, some think of their families. Ceyx calls to Alcyone: he yearns to turn toward the coast of his home-land but no longer knows in which direction he'll find it. A whirling storm cloud lashes the mast and shatters it, and the tiller, too; an immense breaker smashes into the ship and sinks it. The men are submerged. Ceyx holds onto a piece of the wreckage, prays to Lucifer and Aeolus, but thinks above all of Alcyone, hoping that the waves will carry his body to her. He utters her name, murmuring it amid the waves; then a black mass of water rises up above the waves and plunges down over his head, and the sea closes over him.

In the meantime, unaware of all this, Alcyone prays to Juno for her husband's return. But the goddess, tired of being invoked for a dead man, sends her messenger Iris to tell Sleep to give Alcyone a dream of Ceyx dead, so that she'll understand the truth. Here a secondary but powerful perspective opens in the narration: for the first time in liter-ature, Ovid describes, brilliantly, Sleep's dwelling in the land of the Cimmerians, a cave with deep crannies, immersed in fogs and a vague twilight glow. *Muta quies habitat*: every-thing here is silence and peace, except for the stream of Lethe that slides over the pebbles and counsels sleep. The god lies languidly on a bed of feathers, asleep. Around him are the "empty" dreams: countless as the grains of sand on the beach. Iris enters, manages to wake Sleep enough to get him to understand Juno's message and send Alcyone his son Morpheus, *artificem simulatoremque figurae*: the artist and simulator of form, the perfect mimic of every figure, who knows better than anyone else how to assume the features—face, speech, gait, clothes—of a human being.

Morpheus changes himself into Ceyx: a livid, naked corpse, beard soaked, hair dripping, he appears to poor sleeping Alcyone, asks her to recognize him, and tells her he died in a shipwreck:

"Do you know me, your Ceyx? Am I changed
In death? Look! Now you see, you recognize—
Ah! not your husband but your husband's ghost.
Your prayers availed me nothing. I am dead.
Feed not your heart with hope, hope false and vain.
A wild sou'wester in the Aegean sea,
Striking my ship, in its huge hurricane
Destroyed her. Over my lips, calling your name—
Calling in vain—the waters washed. These tidings
No dubious courier brings, no vague report:
Myself, here, shipwrecked, my own fate reveal.
Come, rise and weep! Put on your mourning! Weep!
Nor unlamented suffer me to join
The shadowy spirits of the Underworld."

Still asleep, Alcyone weeps, trying to embrace her husband's body; she wakes, looks around for him, tears her clothes and her hair, and to her nurse, who has rushed in to find out what's going on, she cries: "'Alcyone's no more, no more!' she cried. 'She died with Ceyx, died when Ceyx died! / Give me no words of comfort—he is dead, / Shipwrecked and drowned. I saw him, knew him, tried /

To hold him—as he vanished—in my arms. / He was a ghost, but yet distinct and clear, / Truly my husband's ghost.'"

It's morning now: Alcyone goes to the beach, to the place where she watched the ship's departure; she recalls the details of the farewell and suddenly she sees floating on the water something she can't distinguish. When the object comes closer, driven by the waves, she sees that it's a body. Alcyone is stricken with pity. The body comes even closer: distraught, she recognizes it—it's her husband. She cries: *Ille est* (It's him), and holds out her trembling hands, saying: "'Is this . . . my dearest love, is this—So piteous—how you come home to me!'" Next to her is a pier: she jumps up to it, but it's not a human leap: she's flying now, and: "She flew and through the air on new-found wings / Sped skimming o'er the waves, a hapless bird." Her mouth emits a squeaking sound, like a grieving lament; when she reaches the body she enfolds it in her wings and, her beak now hard, tries to cover it with kisses. Perhaps Ceyx feels those kisses, or maybe it's the motion of the waves that makes him seem to raise his face toward her. There, he feels them: *superis miserantibus*—through the gods' pity—both are changed to birds. And their love continues, even now that they're birds: the *foedus coniugiale*, the marriage bond, still binds. The halcyon and the kingfisher mate, proliferate. For seven days, in winter, Alcyone sits in a nest suspended high above the water: "Calm lies the sea." Aeolus holds the winds prisoner and forbids them to go out, offering his grandchildren a tranquil sea.

Thus we return to the halcyons and the kingfisher, and the flight skimming over the crest of the waves. We have, in fact, found the mythical roots of the kingfisher's flight. Ovid's remarkable story aims, in a certain sense, precisely at that, based on the etiology of the halcyon days that in early December allow kingfishers to nest.

Yet it's as a narrative that we have to examine the myth. And here we can say only that the flight of the kingfisher originates in a desperate grief, in the separation of death finally recognized in the physical body, whereas the flight of the male and the female, of the kingfisher as a species, flourishes in a love that endures after death. Ovid's story, as we've seen, repeatedly emphasizes the love between Ceyx and Alcyone. A love that joins two human beings and two elements, the light that announces day—the morning star, Lucifer, father of Ceyx—and the kingdom of the winds: Aeolus, father of Alcyone. It is in fact between light and wind, in the air, that flight unfolds.

But the narrative is both more complex and simpler than what this allegory might indicate. First Ceyx leaves his wife: in spite of the emotion he feels at her words, the man leaves her to go and consult an unspecified oracle. He tears the fabric of the marriage bond to pursue a vague thirst for knowledge. Yet he exists only as the husband of Alcyone: as soon as he abandons her, he dies. The terrible storm that drowns him is also regenerating: through the metamorphosis dictated by love and divine compassion, Ceyx rises from it in the guise of a kingfisher. In that sense, the terrifying Ovidian storm is the ancestor, the *typos,* of the storm in Shakespeare: in *Twelfth Night*, in *Pericles*, in *The Tempest*. But Alcyone, too, as she herself declares, can't live without her husband, and she, too, has to have the experience of death in order to be reborn as a bird. Alcyone has to descend into the abyss three times: first, in the foreboding anguish that she feels from the start at the idea of her husband going on a journey by sea; then, when Morpheus appears to her in a dream as Ceyx drowned; finally, as his body slowly approaches the shore.

Alcyone's recognition of death is twofold: in the first place, of the shade, of the image of her husband that Morpheus, the maker of shapes, embodies for her in the dream. Alcyone's dream is the equivalent of Ceyx's storm: in the storm he continues to murmur words addressed to her, in the dream she speaks to him, weeping. The two realities, of the dream and of the events, are presented on the same plane. But while on the plane of events the storm puts an end to life, to existence itself, on the other the nightmare generates actions that lead to a metamorphosis. The one, therefore, takes up and continues the other.

The Ovidian story is in fact a specular sequence—that is, a narrative in which the two central characters, bound to one another by a great love and so virtually a single thing, diffract in a mirror, which in turn reflects their image in another mirror, and so on up to the moment when everything is about to shatter. Alcyone leaps onto the pier evidently intending to throw herself into the sea to reach the dead body of her husband. At that precise instant, she is transfigured: the suicidal leap—*mirum*, most wonderful—becomes flight, and flight as a condition of being: *volabat, stringebat*—the imperfects suggest an enduring state. Alcyone, however, preserves human affections intact: already a bird, she seeks Ceyx, explores his body, wraps it in her arms that have become wings, tries to kiss him. And the kiss revives him, transforms him—as Shakespeare would say—"into something rich and strange." Ovid is attentive to the crucial point: "Whether he felt them or the lapping waves Raised Ceyx' head, folk doubted." The spectator is suddenly summoned to the scene, like the audience (*populus*) in a theater, and on him the poet confers the doubt of each of us.

It's a moment at which everything could shatter. *At ille senserat*, Ovid responds, with immense faith in the redemption that poetry can suggest: "Yet he felt them." Beyond death and its unmaking, beyond the bird's hard beak, Ceyx feels: the bloated and shapeless mass, the formless no-longer-a-being, perceives the presence and the love. The mirror is reconstructed in a living being. In the dream, Morpheus had the livid, naked corpse say: "Myself, here, shipwrecked, my own fate reveal." Now, after the metamorphosis, the narrator himself observes: "The same strange fate / They shared, and still their love endured."

This is precisely the root of our myth as narrative: the flight of the kingfisher conceals a very simple and powerful message. It celebrates the union of male and female—of man and woman—and the perpetuation of the species. It exalts the capacity of the female, the woman, to nourish and save the male, the man. There is nothing, for humanity, for every human being, that goes deeper to the heart of innate instincts. The flight of the kingfishers sings *life*. It may be the poetry of small things, perhaps even consoling, but it is *human* poetry.

And perhaps something more, because it celebrates the

persistence of life, again thanks to the female, after death. It's pointless to hide behind the dream and the metamorphosis, although they are also deeply, radically necessary for the artist, like a Morpheus, to create his shapes: both speak of continuity, in the psyche the first, in the body the second: in the spirit and in the flesh. The medieval allegorizers,such as the anonymous author of *L'Ovide moralisé* and Bersuire, had no difficulty speaking of the soul as the bride of Christ. "When she," the former writes, "sees her husband embark on the ship and the journey during which he is overwhelmed by a storm and dies; when she sees him and thinks him dead, she, too, has to go into the sea, that is, out of devotion in the bitterness of repentance and confession; and when he is resurrected and ascends as a bird, she herself has to be renewed, and through contemplation ascend and fly."

In any case, the message in Ovid's story is clear: and the love that joins woman and man will be celebrated, under the guise of Alcyone and Ceyx, by Chaucer, Gower, and Christine de Pizan in the Middle Ages, by Dryden at the end of the seventeenth century, and by Maurice Ravel at the start of the twentieth. Even the Romantic Coleridge praises it as an icon of domestic peace.

Ovid was exiled by Augustus; we still don't know why, and perhaps never will. He spent a good part of his life in Tomis, on the Black Sea, and probably he composed, or finished composing, the *Metamorphoses* there. Far from Rome, far from the literary glory he could have had, far from friends, from loves: far from civilization. Yet in that remote place, amid the barbarians, Ovid wrote immortal poetry, which he sent regularly to Rome and which was regularly published, because Augustus wasn't a fool: he couldn't tolerate Ovid for who knows what reason—maybe political, maybe because Ovid had spoken ill of some member of the imperial family—but his poems were extraordinarily beautiful, and so they circulated freely in Rome and the rest of the Empire. Ovid knew it, and he knew that the *Metamorphoses*, the most unexpected and original work of antiquity, would create its own space as a classic, would be affirmed overwhelmingly outside the established canons of genre: that it was a work and a world capable of crossing the confines of time.

Ovid knew that he had composed a work that would last forever: like the essence and fame of Rome. So he tells us in conclusion, having recounted, in the last two books, the mythical story of the city, and narrated the final metamorphosis, of Julius Caesar into a comet, and celebrated Augustus, and evoked that Pythagoras who returns to the cosmogony of Book I and announces the very philosophy of the poem: "Nothing dies in the entire world, but it changes and transforms its aspect."

With this I would like to conclude my series of lectures on the classics, because Ovid seems to indicate that ancient poetry will continue and come down—at least—to our times:

Now stands my task accomplished, such a work
As not the wrath of Jove, nor fire nor sword
Nor the devouring ages can destroy.
Let, when it will, that day, that has no claim
But to my mortal body, end the span
Of my uncertain years. Yet I'll be borne,

The finer part of me, above the stars,
Immortal, and my name shall never die.
Wherever through the lands beneath her sway
The might of Rome extends, my words shall be
Upon the lips of men. If truth at all
Is stablished by poetic prophecy,
My fame shall live to all eternity.

NOTES

[1] Homer, *The Iliad*, translated by Robert Fagles (New York: Penguin Books, 1990). All citations from the *Iliad* are from this edition.

[2] Longinus, *On the Sublime*, in *Classical Literary Criticism*, translated by Penelope Murray and T. S. Dorsch (London: Penguin Books, 2000). All citations from Longinus are from this edition.

[3] Rachel Bespaloff, *On the Iliad*, translated by Mary McCarthy (New York: Pantheon Books, 1947).

[4] Jacqueline de Romilly, *Hector* (Editions de Fallois, 1997). Translated from the Italian by Ann Goldstein.

[5] Matteo Nucci, *Le lacrime degli eroi* (Torino: Einaudi Editore, 2013).

[6] Homer, *The Odyssey*, translated by Richmond Lattimore (New York: Harper & Row, 1967). All citations from the *Odyssey* are from this edition.

[7] Cicero, *On Ends*, translated by H. Rackham (Loeb Classical Library, Cambridge, MA: Harvard University Press, 1914).

[8] Pietro Citati, *La mente colorata. Ulisse e l'Odissea* (Milano: Mondadori, 2002).

[9] Hesiod, *Theogony and Works and Days*, translated by M. L. West (Oxford and New York: Oxford University Press, 2008). All citations from *Theogony and Works and Days* are from this edition.

[10] Bruno Snell, *Die Entdeckung des Geistes* (Hamburg: Claaszen & Coverts Verlag, 1946). Translated from the Italian by Ann Goldstein.

[11] Giorgio Colli, *La nascita della filosofia* (Milano: Adelphi, 1975).

[12] Marcel Detienne, *The Masters of Truth in Archaic Greece*, translated by Janet Lloyd (Cambridge, MA: Zone Books, 1996).

[13] Aristotle, *Metaphysics*, translated and with an introduction by Hugh Lawson-Tancred (New York: Penguin Books, 1998).

[14] *Early Greek Philosophy*, Volume V, edited and translated by André Laks and Glenn W. Most (Loeb Classical Library, Cambridge, MA: Harvard University Press, 2016).

[15] *Ibid.*

[16] Heracleitus, *On the Universe*, in *Hippocrates Volume IV*, translated by W. H. S. Jones (Loeb Classical Library, Cambridge, MA: Harvard University Press, 1931). All citations from Heraclitus are from this volume.

[17] Aristotle, *Athenian Constitution. Eudemian Ethics. Virtues and Vices*. Translated by H. Rackham (Loeb Classical Library, Cambridge, MA: Harvard University Press, 1935).

[18] Euripides, *Fragments*, edited and translated by Christopher Collard and Martin Cropp (Loeb Classical Library, Cambridge, MA: Harvard University Press, 2008).

[19] Lucretius, *On the Nature of the Universe*, translated by Ronald Melville (Oxford and New York: Oxford University Press, 1997). All citations from Lucretius are from this edition.

[20] Aeschylus, *Prometheus Bound and Other Plays*, translated and with an introduction by Philip Vellacott (London: Penguin Books, 1961). All citations from *Prometheus Bound* are from this edition.

[21] Herodotus, *The Histories*, translated by Aubrey de Sélincourt; revised with introduction and notes by John Marincola (London and New York: Penguin Books, 1996). All citations from Herodotus are from this edition.

[22] Thucydides, *The Peloponnesian War*, translated by Martin Hammond (Oxford and New York: Oxford University Press, 2009). All citations from Thucydides are from this edition.

[23] *Aeschylus II: The Oresteia*, translated by Richmond Lattimore (Chicago: The University of Chicago Press, 2013). All citations from the *Oresteia* are from this edition.

[24] Seneca, *Tragedies*, edited and translated by John G. Fitch

(Loeb Classical Library, Cambridge, MA: Harvard University Press, 2018).

²⁵ Sophocles, *The Theban Plays* (*Oedipus the King, Oedipus at Colonus, Antigone*), translated by E. F. Watling (London: Penguin Books, 1947). All citations from *The Theban Plays* are from this edition.

²⁶ *The Portable Plato: Protagoras, Symposium, Phaedo, and the Republic*, translated by Benjamin Jowett; edited and with an introduction by Scott Buchanan (New York: Viking Press, 1948).

²⁷ Euripides, *The Suppliants*, translated by George Theodoridis (Creative Commons © 2010).

²⁸ Sophocles, *Electra and Other Plays*, translated by E. F. Watling (London: Penguin Books, 1953). All citations from *Electra* are from this edition.

²⁹ Plato, *The Last Days of Socrates: Euthyphro, Apology, Crito, Phaedo*, translated by Hugh Tredennick and Harold Tarrant (London: Penguin Books, 1993). All citations from *Apology, Crito, and Phaedo* are from this edition.

³⁰ *Plato's Cosmology: The Timaeus of Plato*, translated by Francis Macdonald Cornford (London: Routledge, 1935). All citations from *Timaeus* are from this edition.

³¹ Aristotle, *The Nicomachean Ethics*, translated by J. A. K. Thomson, revised by Hugh Tredennick (London: Penguin Books, 1976).

³² *Greek Lyric Poetry*, translated by M. L. West (Oxford and New York: Oxford University Press, 1993). Except where indicated, all translations in this chapter are from this volume.

³³ *The Greek Anthology, Volume III, Book 9*, translated by W. R. Paton (Loeb Classical Library, Cambridge, MA: Harvard University Press, 1917).

³⁴ *Ibid*. M.L. West.

³⁵ Translation Piero Boitani. Translated from the Italian by Ann Goldstein.

³⁶ Pindar, *The Complete Odes*, translated by Anthony Verity (Oxford and New York: Oxford University Press, 2007). All citations from Pindar are from this edition.

[37] Polybius, *The Rise of the Roman Empire*, translated by Ian Scott-Kilvert; selected with an introduction by F. W. Walbank (London: Penguin Books, 1979).

[38] Cicero, *The Republic*, translated by Clinton W. Keyes (Loeb Classical Library, Cambridge MA: Harvard University Press, 1928).

[39] Virgil, *Aeneid*, translated by Allen Mandelbaum (New York: Bantam Dell, 2003). All citations from the *Aeneid* are from this edition.

[40] Sallust, *The War with Catiline, The War with Jugurtha*, translated by J. C. Rolfe (Loeb Classical Library, Cambridge, MA: Harvard University Press, 2013). All citations from these works are from this edition.

[41] Tacitus, *Annals*, translated and with an introduction by Cynthia Damon (London: Penguin Classics, 2012). All citations from the *Annals* are from this edition.

[42] Tacitus, *Agricola*, translated by M. Hutton, revised by R. M. Ogilvie (Loeb Classical Library, Cambridge, MA: Harvard University Press, 1970). All citations from *Agricola* are from this edition.

[43] Tacitus, *The Annals and The Histories*, translated by Alfred John Church and William Jackson Brodribb (New York: Modern Library, 2003). All citations from the *Histories* are from this edition.

[44] C. Julius Caesar, *Caesar's Gallic War*, translated by W. A. McDevitte and W. S. Bohn (New York: Harper & Brothers, 1869).

[45] Sallust, *Fragments of the Histories*, edited and translated by John T. Ramsey (Loeb Classic Library, Cambridge, MA: Harvard University Press, 2015).

[46] Ovid, *Metamorphoses*, translated by A. D. Melville (Oxford and New York: Oxford University Press, 1998). All translations from the *Metamorphoses* are from this edition.

Index of Names

ABOUT THE AUTHOR

Piero Boitani is one of Italy's most renowned literary critics. An expert on ancient myths, a medievalist, and a Dante scholar, he is currently a Professor of Comparative Literature at the Sapienza University in Rome.